OXFORD
INDIA SHORT
INTRODUCTIONS

DALIT ASSERTION

The Oxford India Short
Introductions are concise,
stimulating, and accessible guides
to different aspects of India.
Combining authoritative analysis,
new ideas, and diverse perspectives,
they discuss subjects which are
topical yet enduring, as also
emerging areas of study and debate.

OTHER TITLES IN THE SERIES

The Indian Constitution
Madhav Khosla

Natural Disasters and Indian History
Tirthankar Roy

Caste
Surinder S. Jodhka

The Poverty Line
S. Subramanian

Indian Cities
Annapurna Shaw

Monetary Policy
Partha Ray

The Right to Information in India
Sudhir Naib

Affirmative Action in India
Ashwini Deshpande

Water Resources of India
A. Vaidyanathan

Panchayati Raj
Kuldeep Mathur

Trade and Environment
Rajat Acharyya

The Civil Services in India
S.K. Das

Capital Flows and Exchange Rate Management
Soumyen Sikdar

OXFORD
INDIA SHORT
INTRODUCTIONS

DALIT ASSERTION

SUDHA PAI

OXFORD
UNIVERSITY PRESS

OXFORD
UNIVERSITY PRESS

Oxford University Press is a department of the University of Oxford.
It furthers the University's objective of excellence in research, scholarship,
and education by publishing worldwide. Oxford is a registered trademark of
Oxford University Press in the UK and in certain other countries

Published in India by
Oxford University Press
22 Workspace, 2nd Floor, 1/22 Asaf Ali Road, New Delhi 110002, India

© Oxford University Press 2013

The moral rights of the author have been asserted

First Edition published in 2013

Digitally Printed in 2025

ISBN-13: 978-0-19-809593-4
ISBN-10: 0-19-809593-7

Typeset in 11/15.6 Bembo Std
by Excellent Laser Typesetters, Pitampura, Delhi 110 034
Printed in India by Manipal Technologies Limited, Manipal

Contents

Preface and Acknowledgements

Over the last three decades, India has experienced a strong wave of Dalit assertion with significant implications for the working of our democracy. An upsurge from below by social groups that have historically remained oppressed and marginalized is a product of democratization in the post-Independence period. Dalit assertion has taken a number of forms; in this short introduction three contemporary forms are discussed: grass roots assertion, political parties, and middle class activism. Dalits, through their social and political activities, have constructed a new identity of the Dalit and an alternative ideology to Brahminism, and challenged structures of inequality and hierarchy. This has been the result of efforts by a newly educated post-Independence generation which is no longer willing to put up with oppression. This has led to a backlash, resulting in conflict and considerable violence, particularly from the upwardly mobile Backward Castes who today constitute the direct oppressors of the Dalits in many regions. At the same time, the nature and form of Dalit assertion has been a source of considerable controversy. While it is correctly argued that it has contributed to the social deepening of democracy, questions have been raised about whether it has actually helped the vast majority of subaltern Dalits. This short introduction attempts to provide an understanding of the emergence and various facets of Dalit assertion and its impact on the working of democratic structures and processes: local power structures, electoral politics, and globalization. It highlights the achievements of Dalit assertion, but also discusses its weaknesses, limitations, and possibilities.

This short introduction is the product of many years of teaching and research on this area and many questions raised here have emerged from classroom discussions and some excellent term papers and M. Phil theses written by students. This is really a work for my students and is based on what I have learnt from them. A large number of students, colleagues, friends, and scholars have contributed to the ideas contained here, whom I would be unable to thank individually. I hope it will be of interest to the general reader too. While the general reader is often familiar with the ideas and even the workings of our democracy, most of them do not encounter the hopes, demands, and assertions of those who are disadvantaged and marginalized. If this book helps raise social sensitivity about these issues among the general reader, it would have fulfilled its purpose. Finally, I would like to thank the editorial team at Oxford University Press for their efficient and friendly handling of this book.

6 November 2012   SUDHA PAI

Abbreviations

AIADMK	All India Anna Dravida Munnetra Kazhagam
AISCF	All India Scheduled Castes Federation
BAMCEF	The All India Backward (SC, ST, and OBC) and Minority Communities Employees' Federation
BC	Backward Class
BD	Bhopal Document
BJP	Bharatiya Janata Party
BRPI	Bharatiya Republican Party of India
BSP	Bahujan Samaj Party
CMP	Common Minimum Programme
CPI (M)	Communist Party of India (Marxist)
DKVF	Devendra Kula Vellalars Federation

DMK	Dravida Munnetra Kazhagam
DP	Dalit Panther
DPI	Dalit Panther Iyakkam
DTIC	District Trade and Industry Centres
FDI	foreign direct investment
FICCI	Federation of Indian Chambers of Commerce and Industry
GDP	gross domestic product
IAS	Indian Administrative Services
IMR	Infant Mortality Rate
INC	Indian National Congress
INL	Indian National League
IT	Information Technology
MBC	Most Backward Class
MTD	Makkal Tamil Desam
NBM	Non-Brahmin Movement
NDA	National Democratic Alliance
NGO	Non-governmental Organization
OBC	Other Backward Class
PD	Protective Discrimination
PMK	Pattali Makal Katchi
PSU	Public Sector Undertaking
PT	Puthiya Tamilagam
RDS	Rani Durgawati Scheme

RPI	Republican Party of India
SAM	Social Action Movement
SC	Scheduled Caste
SCF	Scheduled Caste Federation
SD	Supplier Diversity
SP	Samajwadi Party
SRM	Self-respect Movement
ST	Scheduled Tribe
TAMBRAS	TN Brahmin Association
TMMK	Tamil Muslim Munnetra Kazhagam
TNUEF	Tamil Nadu Untouchability Eradication Front
UP	Uttar Pradesh
UPA	United Progressive Alliance

Introduction

Dalit Assertion, Democratization, and Politics

In the last few decades, India has experienced a strong wave of Dalit assertion. As the product of an upsurge from below, it manifests itself in the socio-economic, cultural, and political realm and has taken many different forms: movements against caste domination, political parties, protest literature, a variety of grassroot assertions, and more recently—middle class activism. Dalit assertion has increased political consciousness, enabled greater political participation of this disadvantaged section, and helped shape the nature and direction of democracy in this country. Such movements have often led to social conflict and violent 'caste atrocities' against Dalits in many parts of the country. The nature and form of Dalit assertion has also been a source of considerable controversy. On the one hand, it has been described as leading to the social deepening of democracy; while on the other questions have been raised about whether it has actually helped the subaltern Dalits.

Dalits are not a homogeneous group and the impact of Dalit assertion has been differential both in terms of sub-castes and region. In a comprehensive review of major works, John Webster has pointed out that the term 'Dalit movement' has been used to describe many similarly placed primordial Dalit collectivities with similar histories of oppression, simultaneously seeking to overcome similar deprivations within a common social system, but with differing visions of their own and society's future (Webster 1995). Many scholars analysing social movements—including the Dalit movement—reveal how difficult it is to give tight definitions or sets of characteristics which do justice to the complexities of many diverse social movements in modern Indian history. (Gorringe 2005; Shah 2000) This suggests that there are many 'Dalit movements', which are region-specific and arose independently at different times in the colonial and post-Independence period, rather than a single movement which developed on the basis of on a common ideology.

While our concern here is with Dalit assertion in the post-Independence period, the process of awakening and increasing political consciousness, undoubtedly began in the colonial period. While the national movement was more concerned with the national than the caste question, Congress leaders, particularly Gandhi tried to address the issue of untouchability and the upliftment of the Depressed Classes—as the Dalits were then known. But strong movements against caste oppression took place during the colonial period under leaders such as B.R. Ambedkar, M.C. Rajah, and Ramaswami Naicker. Ambedkar led a fight against caste discrimination, demanded entry into temples, representation and reservation in politics and in posts in the colonial bureaucracy. Confrontation took place between leaders such as Gandhi and Ambedkar culminating in the Poona Pact of 1932. A legacy of these developments was the provision of protective discrimination for disadvantaged sections in the Constitution of independent India. However, Dalit consciousness—and movements based on it—was limited to only some parts of the subcontinent, arrived late in many regions, and affected only a small number. Consequently, the large majority remained unaffected and trapped in the larger identity of Hindu.

In this book, an attempt has been made to illustrate that Dalit assertion over the last few decades has been both the cause and the consequence of the larger process of democratization in India. Understanding this larger process and using it as a framework of inquiry will allow us to evaluate what assertion has meant for Dalits and for democracy in India. After Independence, India adopted a liberal democracy with a written Constitution that provided a parliamentary system, with both individual and groups rights for Scheduled Caste (SC), Scheduled Tribe (ST), and backward groups. It was to be a path of gradual social transformation that sought to combine the goals of growth and redistribution, while avoiding the violence disruption and regimentation of revolutionary change. Under the leadership of Nehru, commitment to democratic transformation was an integral part of India's developmental strategy and was a unique experiment. But it was an elite democracy in which a large number of citizens, particularly disadvantaged sections including Dalits, did not participate. Democratization can be understood as a gradual, long term, multifaceted process, operating since Independence that has helped marginalized sections of society and polity participate in the process and claim equality with other citizens of the country. The process of democratization has been uneven across the subcontinent. It has proceeded faster in some regions and slower in others and slowly moved; downwards towards more and more subaltern groups. It is an ongoing process that is not yet over. It has not been unilinear in nature—rather it has moved back and forth with setbacks from time to time—and faced challenges which have yet to be fully overcome.

The central argument here is that Dalit assertion—witnessed over the past few decades is a distinctly post-Independence phenomenon—the result of the long term process of democratization in post-Independent India. Assertion in this context means to question or challenge the unequal hierarchical caste structure and the resisting of norms of purity and pollution provided in the *Manusmriti*—a part of the Hindu Dharmshastras—that have placed the Dalit or ex-untouchable at the bottom, below the line of pollution. Dalit assertion therefore is a strident revolt or upsurge from below by the Dalits against being social outcastes. Such a revolt has a distinct meaning for our democracy—it means going beyond normal forms of democratic participation—to movements and actions aimed at breaking down structures of inequality leading to social transformation. Dalit assertion has specific characteristics, such as the construction of Dalit identity and an alternative ideology to Brahminism, which has challenged upper caste hegemony. In some regions of the country—notably southern and western India—this process has its roots in movements against the caste system in the colonial period, such as the non-Brahmin movement and the Mahar movement respectively. In most of the regions of the Hindi heartland, it is a post-Independence phenomenon, which is a result of multifaceted aspects of democratization—such as adoption of a democratic Constitution with protective discrimination and recognition of group rights, adoption of adult franchise with regular free and fair elections, land reform, rise in political consciousness, rise in literacy, improvement in the socio-economic conditions of the lower castes, and a host of associated developments. This explains the inability of the Republican Party of India (RPI) in the 1960s to strike roots and establish itself as a party or movement in a number of states, and the rise of Bahujan Samaj Party (BSP) after nearly 30 years after independence. Similarly, it also explains why it was only in the 1980s that Dalits in Tamil Nadu—who had long supported non-Brahminism——called for a re-examination of Dravidian ideology and moved away to form their own independent identity. Everywhere it was only after considerable democratization had taken place, that a self-given, stronger identity of Dalit could be formed leading to strong social movements against the caste hierarchy. This identity then moved into politics creating Dalit parties and identity-based politics. Hence, a major objective is to trace the process of democratization and its relationship to Dalit assertion in the Hindi heartland, as well as its newer forms in southern and western India. This will throw light upon the forms and features and strengths and weaknesses of Dalit assertion and its resulting impact.

The aim therefore is to understand the nature, form, and direction of Dalit assertion in various regions of the country—each of which has its own specific features. During the colonial period, three ideological forms emerged: Gandhian, Dravidian, and the

Ambedkarite. The first arose in the colonial period and was based on Gandhi's thinking on caste—but after Independence with Dalits supporting the Congress party—came to be associated with Nehruvian India. It lost importance following the decline of the Congress party in the 1980s, providing space for a variety of post-Ambedkarite movements and parties such as the Dalit Panthers, BSP, revival of the RPI, and a host of smaller groups. The Dravidian form is being stridently questioned today by Dalits in Tamil Nadu who are trying to create an independent ideology and identity. Thus a wide variety of ideologies and contemporary movements exist in different regions of the country.

Many distinct strands have also emerged within the Dalit movement. Strong grass roots movements underlie much of the strident assertion witnessed in recent years often leading to confrontational politics, violence, and atrocities. Dalit parties are attempting to capture power and introduce change through Dalit-oriented programmes and policies while also practising the politics of symbolism such as erecting statues, memorials, and renaming districts and roads after Dalit icons. An educated generation of Dalits has introduced middle class activism which has brought a new dimension into

the Dalit movement for social equality. New values
and norms have been formulated; the most important
being social justice which underlies all movements.
The meaning of this term and the promise it holds
out for Dalits is still being debated. More recently, with
the relative weakening of identity politics—demands
for rapid economic development point to the gradual
emergence of a post-identity phase in the Dalit movement, particularly in the Hindi heartland—the con-
tours of which are just beginning to be understood.
While caste has not lost importance, a new combination of caste and developmental issues has emerged
which could affect the carefully built consolidated
support base of Dalit parties in the future.

Due to these developments, scholars have argued
that while movements based on assertion in the post-
Independence period—whether in Tamil Nadu, Uttar
Pradesh, Maharashtra, or Punjab, initially held great
promise and were radical and anti-caste in their outlook—by the close of the 1990s, this early promise
seemed to have lost its edge. They shifted from radical
movements and organizations to being competitive
political parties that have compromised and formed
electoral and governmental alliances with mainstream

political parties and groups, earlier denounced as casteist. Thus, a central question that is being investigated is whether the larger process of democratization, and within it, Dalit assertion has run out of steam? Has the rise of an educated middle class, globalization, and the private sector introduced change in the ideology and mobilizational patterns of the Dalit movement in the country? There has been a shift from strident movements for social transformation to middle class activism—leading to demands for extending reservation to the private sector and in higher education, affirmative action in business, the establishment of a Dalit Chamber of Commerce—in order to build a middle class which can participate in the economy and polity so that Dalits can also gain a share in the fruits of post-Independence development. In this scenario, issues such as removal of untouchability, caste atrocities, and social equality have become less important.

Paradoxically, this has happened precisely when Dalit parties have become strong, but their sights are now fixed on capturing power and bringing in change from above rather than a long struggle at the grass roots to bring about social transformation. The downward movement of Dalit assertion, empowering the smaller, poorer and marginalized sub-castes evident during the 1990s, seems to have slowed down as capturing power has become more important. Nor have sub-caste divisions been overcome; also classification of caste has further divided Dalit groups. Yet at the same time, assertion at the grass roots remains strong in states where Dalits have attempted to challenge upper caste domination. This is seen in the installation of Ambedkar statues, formation of Dalit organizations in villages and cities, circulation of Dalit literature in the form of small books and pamphlets in the countryside, revolt against atrocities by *savarna* Hindus, and anger and violence against the practice of untouchability. Does this explain the lack of a single Dalit movement throughout the country? Should different movements be understood and examined differently? These are some of the questions that this study raises and attempts to answer. For this, an understanding of the nature of democratization is needed because answers, perhaps, lie embedded in the type of democratic structures, processes, and values that Indian democracy has thrown up.

Democratization: Concept and Indian Specificity

The concept of 'democratization' refers to political changes moving in a democratic direction. The term in social science literature has been used to compare the process over time and across states in the world beginning with north-west Europe. Samuel Huntington points to three long waves of democratization beginning with north-west Europe in the mid-1800s; reaching southern Europe in the 1900s, and then a third wave which marked the post-colonial world following decolonization (Huntington 1991). In more recent times it has affected Eastern Europe and the Soviet Union. The character of this change over time is from less accountable to more accountable government, from less competitive elections to freer and fairer competitive elections, from severely restricted to better protected civil and political rights, and from weak autonomous associations in civil society to more autonomous and more numerous associations (Potter *et al.* 1997). Some states move in this direction—others do not—or gradually do so.

Democratization is a complex and multifaceted process, with different historical trajectories, that no single theoretical approach can completely capture and explain satisfactorily. Three theoretical approaches have attempted to explain its features and forms. The modernization approach emphasized on social and economic requisites, such as rising per capita income and literacy necessary for successful democratization (Lipset 1994). The transition approach, developed particularly from analysis of Latin American experiences, emphasizes on political processes and elite initiatives that lead from authoritarian to liberal democracy (Rustow 1970). The structural approach emphasizes changing structures of power favourable to democratization (Moore 1996). The first two are more suited to countries that are not yet democratic, or are making the transition to democracy. It is the third that could be useful for understanding democratization in India, where the explanatory focus is on long-term processes of historical change—the process of democratization is explained not by the agency of political elites but primarily by changing structures of power. A good example is Barrington Moore (1996) writing on the

shift from agrarian landlordism to commercial agriculture, and finally industrial society and liberal democracy
under a bourgeoisie which has emerged as the dominant class in society. Rueschmeyer *et al.* (1992) focus
on the growth of the working class and the industrial
proletariat and how they play a role in democratization. These studies point out that historically the state
apparatus separated, at least to some extent, from the
array of classes in society has been a prerequisite for
democratization and demands from subordinate classes
being successfully accommodated and implemented. A
very powerful and almost autonomous state in relation
to social classes and groups has provided a most uncon-
genial setting for democratization. Rather, democracy has had a greater chance in the middle ground
between absent and excess state power. Political parties
and active civil society has succeeded in providing a
counterweight to state power.

India: Specificity and Context

The existing literature on democratization, discussed
above, cannot claim explanatory universality and, particularly, does not adequately help in explaining the

Indian situation. What is required is to understand the historical uniqueness and context of democratization. India does not fit neatly into either the modernization or dependency approaches in comparative analysis. In many countries of Latin America, Africa, or Asia—democratization means moving from military or authoritarian rule to democracy, that is, the introduction and establishment of democratic structures and values within society.

However, India adopted a model of liberal democracy at Independence—has never experienced military rule—and saw only a brief period of authoritarianism during the Emergency (1975–7). Democratization means creating more space for the inclusion of various marginalized sections into the polity and society. The existing literature recognizes that class divisions are not the only form of social inequality. Other group divisions exist on the basis of ethnicity, race, caste, language, tribe, or other cultural criteria. While in western countries class divisions have overridden ethnic divisions this is not the case in India, where caste remains an important social divide. The nature of the state, the extent of its general power in relation to class divisions and or civil society is also an important factor in democracy. The balance of power between the state and social classes, particularly the better-off sections, and a robust civil society is essential for the consolidation and maintenance of liberal democracy. As caste is a key determinant of the social divide, it means challenging its hierarchical structures and creating a more equal society. However, the process of democratization needs to be examined as more than the challenge from below—it should also include the processes that made this possible. It is here that the theories about democratization could perhaps help in the analysis of the Indian variant.

Decolonization after a long period of anti-colonial struggle and the adoption of a democratic federal Constitution set into motion the twin forces of democratization and regionalization (Pai 2000: 5). Democratization has been accompanied by regionalization as India is a large country with many diverse regions. The establishment of a federal structure and of linguistic states provided the states with constitutional, political, and cultural autonomy which helped the states construct a linguistic-cultural identity of their own. The process of state-led economic development, planning, and the goals of equitable growth were conceived as part of this process of gradual democratization of state and civil society. It is the product of a number of developments: the inauguration of the Constitution, adoption of adult franchise, land reforms, spread of literacy, movements, and rise in political awareness. Democratization has been instrumental in the politicization and mobilization of new and underprivileged social groups into politics, assertion of ethnic and regional identities, and movements based upon caste, community, and region. The parallel process of regionalization underlies the gradual shift of power from a single centre to many poles located in the states, though this has not been a continuous process—the balance of power has shifted back and forth over time (Pai 2000: 5). A multi-dimensional process, it is the consequence of the rise of regional consciousness, spread of the electoral process, socio-political mobilization, emergence of identities, and shift to a multi-party system.

These twin processes accelerated in the 1980s due to many socio-economic changes. The decade witnessed the rise of regional or state parties, identity politics, increased politicization, and rise in voter turnout during elections. For the first time, at the all-India level, definite structural shifts and decline in poverty were observed, with substantial decline between 1978 and 1983 (Patnaik and Patnaik 2001). Expansion of public expenditures—especially in rural areas during 1985 to 1990, the Seventh Plan period—in rural areas, power generation, and transport exceeded the revised Plan estimates by a good one-fifth. These expenditures specifically affecting (wholly or partly) the rural areas were 65 per cent of total actual expenditures—and as a proportion of average Gross Domestic Product (GDP) over the period—were at a historic high of about 13.3 per cent compared to the planned level of only 7.8 per cent. There was decline of the overall Infant Mortality Rate (IMR) from 129 to 89 by 1990 and further to 74 by 1994. Life expectancy nearly doubled to 61. Four years for females and 61.1 years for males by 1994; the literacy rate for adults which was abysmally low at Independence, rose to 51 per cent by 1994 (Ibid.). These developments underpinned the rise of Dalit assertion and revolt against upper caste domination.

Dalit Identity: Emergence and Meaning

Dalit assertion has been a significant component in this larger process of democratization after Independence.

The emergence of the identity of Dalit among Scheduled Castes has introduced far reaching changes internally within the Dalit community, its relationship with other caste groups, and impacted society and polity. In the colonial period the term Dalit was not in use. The colonial authorities used the term 'Depressed Classes' in order to avoid other demeaning terms such as *Panchamma* or *Achut* (Gupta 1985) and provided a common identity to this group vis-à-vis the caste Hindus all over the country for the first time. This development was responsible for the beginning of political consciousness among them and movements against caste which increased over time with mobilization by Dalit leaders such as Ambedkar. In contrast, Gandhi introduced the term *Harijan* in the 1920s (literally, children of God). It was based on a traditional concept of a Varna system, cleansed of untouchability, in which untouchables would be 'Harijans', their unclean work made honourable. It has been criticized as a condescending term under which the Indian National Congress (INC) adopted a model of harijan uplift or *uddhar* that continued into the post-colonial period creating a patron–client relationship. Intensely disliked by Dalits, the nomenclature of Harijan was

finally declared unconstitutional through an executive
order of the Government of India in 1991. The term
Scheduled Caste (SC) created under the 1935 Act
became a legal and administrative connotation, and is
associated with the protective discrimination policies
of the post-Independence state.

In sharp contrast, the term Dalit, a value-loaded
term, is qualitatively different and underlies the strong
assertion witnessed since the mid-1980s. Unlike earlier
terms it is 'self-given' and has provided Dalits confidence to reject the inequities of the caste system and
the Gandhian notion of Harijan, and uplift and develop
self-respect, dignity, and pride in low caste identity that
did not exist earlier. Widely used as a form of self-
identification in many parts of the country, sections
such as the *Chamar-Jatav*s of Uttar Pradesh argue that
it is an identity that places them outside the Hindu
community. The most extreme form of rejection was
seen in the conversion to Buddhism. However, the
term holds different meanings for different groups. The
Dalit Panthers in their 1972 Manifesto defined Dalits
broadly in class terms as 'a member of SC and tribes,
neo-Buddhist (the Dalit converts to Buddhists in post-
Independent India), the working people, the landless

and poor peasants, women, and all those who are being exploited politically, economically and, in the name of religion'. Noted Maharashtrian Dalit writer Gangadhar Pantwane argues, 'Dalit is not a caste; Dalit is a symbol of change and revolution. The Dalit believes in humanism. He rejects existence of god, rebirth of soul, sacred books that teach discrimination, fate, and heaven, because these have made him a slave.' Baburao Bagul of the Dalit Panthers has also held it is a category, historically constructed through the revolutionary struggle of the Dalits, and which connotes a desire to change an exploitative society. It is therefore indicative of social and economic oppression. In contrast Dalit identity in the Hindi heartland is not the product of a radical ideology nor does it call for a revolution or struggle— it is a product of economic development, education, affirmative action, and the process of democratization. In fact the broader term, Bahujan which includes the backward castes or classes and the Dalits, was sought to be used by Kanshi Ram initially—but due to differences between the two groups, the narrower term Dalit was finally used. However, sections of Dalits belonging to the middle class are critical of the identity 'Dalit' as they feel it carries the demeaning burden of historical oppression and humiliation. They prefer Buddhist and/ or Ambedkarite as alternatives which, in the process, leaves out the non-Buddhist Dalits (Guru 2009).

Dalit Movement: Impasse or Transition

A recent study has held that the upsurge of Dalit and Other Backward Caste groups and construction of lower caste identities and movements has resulted in 'a seismic shift in patterns of political participation and structures of power' (Lakha and Taneja 2009: 317). A growing literature has documented the significant advances that the Dalit movement has made, at least in pockets since the colonial period, and the central role it is playing in the society and polity. The Dalit community has become politically conscious of its rights and it can collectively challenge, at least at the theoretical level, Brahminical ideology of hierarchy based on pollution and purity. There is an overall acceptance of equality as a desirable norm by a grow-ing number of citizens, thanks to the permeation of a liberal philosophical discourse. Capitalist development to some extent has weakened the traditional function-ing of the caste system; making it a limiting rather than determining factor, and occupational diversification—albeit to a limited extent—has taken place within the Dalit community and globalization could accelerate the process. Protective discrimination, through reservations in government jobs and admission to educational institutions, has created an influential and vocal Dalit middle class creating hope and confidence that there is scope for improving their condition—though the recent process of retreat of the state has begun to affect them adversely. Competitive politics within the parliamentary framework has created greater political consciousness among the Dalits—political leaders with a skill at bargaining in order to manipulate and pressurize the ruling elite have emerged at all levels—from the village panchayat to Parliament. Finally, violence and caste atrocities against Dalits have become less, though have not completely disappeared.

Nevertheless, some scholars have argued that the Dalit movement, which showed great promise in the 1980s and 1990s—has not reached a dead end—but an impasse, that is, a position from which further movement seems difficult (Shah 2001: 13). Shah holds that this impasse is perceptible in both struggles of agitation and parliamentary politics, including elections, and holding offices in various decision making institutions. Despite much agitation and struggle by Dalit leaders in civil society, the hierarchical social structure and attitude of upper castes remains largely unchanged—untouchability is still practised and atrocities against Dalits continue unabated. According to Shah, the Dalit movement has been reduced to a pressure group with its revolutionary edge getting blunted—its strategies, tactics, alliances, and even goals seem to be in dispute. Similarly, despite provision of reserved seats, Dalits have not been able to make a mark in parliament—they occupy office but lack the necessary political power to improve their socio-economic condition. Electoral politics has its own dynamics and cost; the BSP has entered into manipulative politics and opportunistic alliances with upper caste parties. Political leaders get co-opted by the dominant ruling class, partly tempted by higher offices—they share the ideology and agenda of the ruling classes or are unable to find an alternative path (Shah 2001: 13).

Undoubtedly, these developments have disappointed supporters of the Dalit movement and been critiqued by scholars. The BSP, it has been pointed out believes in introducing change from above using state power, rather than a lengthy and difficult movement aimed at social transformation. Consequently, democratization which was moving downwards to include the poorer sub-castes has slowed down (Pai 2002). Dalit parties in Tamil Nadu and Maharashtra, as this study shows, have joined hands with mainstream parties to capture state power and thereby hope to improve social relations. Hugo Gorringe (2005; 2010) argues that the more fundamental problem is that the Dalit movement, almost throughout India, has shifted from 'successful social mobilization to political institutionalization' in the form of parties, which has blunted the edge of the movement. Examining how and why this transition takes place, he feels, is essential for understanding the process of democratization and its impact on social exclusion. Social movement theorists, he holds, have long argued that electoral competition and success is the end goal of movements that challenge existing norms in society (Jenkins and Klandermans 1995; Tarrow 1998). Clause Offe (1990) views institutionalization as an inevitable response to movement 'stagnation' as the initial enthusiasm evaporates and movements 'develop internal organization, become more moderate, adopt a more institutional repertoire of action and integrate into the system of interest representation'. There are benefits he agrees that accrue from this shift, but institutionalized actors may lose the relative autonomy to criticize existing politics and articulate alternatives and they seldom return to the politics of protest. This susceptibility of challenging groups to prioritize continued participation in institutional politics, Gorringe points out, has been described as the 'paradox of collaboration' (Gorringe 2005). However, Gorringe holds quite correctly that the reality probably lies somewhere in between accounts of betrayal of the Dalit movement due to the shift to an opportunistic political party interested in power and an over-positive reading by scholars of electoral results which point to victory of Dalit parties and their ability to introduce change when in office (Ibid.).

This study argues that to understand the changes taking place within the Dalit movement, we need to move beyond Dalit parties and working of institutions and electoral politics to new forms of Dalit assertion that have been more visible in more recent years in some states: Dalit assertion at the grass roots leading to a strong challenge to the power of the landowning middle and backward castes, rise of dalit NGOs and organizations, middle class activism evident in the rising demand for reservation in the private sector and higher education, internationalization of the Dalit movement etc. A basic argument is that the Dalit movement is in a phase of transition—in which it has been able to question with some degree of success—but not been able to overcome upper caste domination and oppression and bring about social transformation. As history shows, transitions can be long, difficult, and involve an element of violence, which is what we are witnessing today. Rather than impasse this phase of the Dalit movement is characterized by a number of strands or dimensions that are impacting society and polity. Many new avenues have opened up which are providing for varied forms of Dalit assertion. Consequently, different forms of assertion co-exist today among the small, but growing middle and lower middle class among Dalits, and the poorer sections—with varying degrees of success in different parts of the country.

While many strands have emerged and co-exist, three major strands are analysed in this volume: assertion at the grass roots, Dalit parties and electoral politics, and middle class activism. Each has its own arena, strategies, aims and goals, as well as strengths and weaknesses, and limitations. These dimensions are facets of the larger process of democratization and are causing a cumulative impact on the Dalit movement. These three strands have been selected because it is in these areas that Dalits are playing a key role today. The Dalit movement finds it greatest strength in assertion at the grass roots which underlies the emergence of political consciousness and identities. While there is no large, organized Dalit movement—there are—as our study shows 'million mutinies' at the grass roots against upper caste domination and oppression, and the failure of the state to protect the life and property of Dalits. They are more visible in states such as Uttar Pradesh, Tamil Nadu, and Punjab but have a presence everywhere and have linkages with and contribute in many ways to mainstream Dalit politics. It is debatable whether the shift from movement to party has helped the Dalit movement or if it has been a regressive step in the fight for social transformation. The emergence of Dalit parties has provided political empowerment and infused self-confidence among Dalits in states such as Uttar Pradesh, while at the same time, assertion at the grass roots continues often independently of parties. Simultaneously, a small but influential, educated, and politically conscious Dalit middle class believes that—with new forms of affirmative action and liberalization—new avenues of advancement are available. Dalits should enter the private sector, industry, media, and academia and make their presence felt. However, such actions would help only a tiny but growing educated urban elite and not extend to the large, rural mass of Dalits.

Thus, there are many dimensions of Dalit assertion today, each of which are contributing in different ways. Their emergence has introduced change in the course and character of the Dalit movement in the country. These dimensions are facets of the larger process of democratization. The present study focuses on their impact, the possibilities and the limitations of the Dalit movement.

1

Ideological Strands in the Dalit Movement

Dalit movements from the very beginning have been based on different ideological strands in different parts of the country. These different strands are the product of not just the large size, but also cultural diversities, social and political environment, social movements, and nature of leadership in different regions of the subcontinent—each region in turn having undergone complex processes of social change at different points of time. As a result of these changes, distinct politico-ideological strands and movements emerged during the colonial period. This continued in the post-Independence period, shaping the nature of Dalit assertion and movements in different regions.

Consequently, despite considerable democratization and assertion in many parts of the country, there is today no pan-Indian Dalit ideology, party, or movement. While Dalits everywhere undoubtedly have common goals and aspirations such as removal of untouchability and achieving social equality, their ideas and actions have been determined by the region to which they belong. In Tamil Nadu for example, Dalits share what Pandian (1994b) describes as 'Tamilness', that is, a common regional and cultural Dravidian identity which is juxtaposed with the Aryan north. Dalit ideology and identity is often different in sub-regions within a state, a good example being the rise of a radical Dalit ideology in Telangana, compared to the moderate outlook on the Andhra coast due to differing historical experiences of the Dalits of both regions. Consequently, Dalits in different regions have developed a distinct ideology, and based on it—an identity of their own embedded in the larger culture, politics, and history of the region— which also emerges from their own historical, cultural, socio-economic, and political experiences.

Starting from the colonial period and continuing in the post-Independence period, Dalit movements can be classified on the basis of three major ideological strands: Dravidian, Ambedkarite, and Gandhian that emerged at different points of time in the colonial period (Pai 2002). Kshirsagar's survey of the Dalit movement in colonial India identifies three major phases: 1857–91, 1891–1919, and 1920–56 (Kshirsagar 1994: 375). It was in southern and western India that the beginnings of Dalit consciousness and movements can be found quite early.

The earliest was the Dravidian movement in southern India closely followed by the Ambedkarite movement in western India, both of which were part of the first phase. They put forward a radical ideology in the colonial period but remained largely reformist in nature leading to protest movements. The Gandhian ideology in northern India arrived late and was absent in the first phase due to lack of a reformist impulse, either internal or due to contact with the West. In contrast to the first two, it was pro-conservative resulting in cooption of certain movements/activities by upper caste/class leaders. The resultant ideological strands and movements were shaped by leaders who organized movements, by the nature of mobilization triggered by the national movement, and other cultural and social reform movements in each region. In the post-Independence period, these ideologies have undergone considerable change with the impact of democratic politics. This chapter attempts a typology of ideological strands underlying Dalit movements in the colonial, and more particularly, the post-Independence period. Only a brief theoretical analysis of different ideological positions is provided—the main purpose is to lay the foundation for analysis of the various forms that Dalit assertion and movements have taken in recent decades and their impact on democratic politics and social transformation. This analysis is taken forward in the remaining chapters.

Dravidian and Adi-Dravid

The Tamil-speaking areas of the Madras Presidency witnessed the construction of a Dravidian ideology of non-Brahminism quite early in the colonial period. Based on region, language, and particularly caste, it challenged the privileged position of the Brahmins in the caste hierarchy. However, the conscious construction of a low caste or Adi-Dravid identity predates the political expression of non-Brahminism, which the former supported, beginning in the last quarter of the nineteenth century. It is seen in the writings of depressed class intellectuals such as Ayothidas, Masilimani, and Appaduraiar, and organizations such as Advaitananda Sangh in 1870, the Chakya Buddhist Sangam in the late 1800s, and the Dravida Mahajana Sangam in 1881 which petitioned the colonial government for separate schools and common wells, and work places for the depressed classes (Geetha and Rajadurai 1993: 2091).

Familiar with Hinduism, Buddhism, and Jainism and attracted by the Advaita Vedanta, these intellectuals attempted to criticize Brahminism, using history to construct an alternative intellectual and spiritual tradition for the lower orders. Ayothidas, through his journalistic/polemical tracts, claimed that Buddhism was the religion of the *panchamma*s, the *poorva Tamizhar* or original inhabitants. The degrading term 'pariah' had been imposed upon the panchammas by Aryan Brahmins who, according to Ayothidas, Hinduized Buddhist texts/religion leading to its decline. Those who agreed to the deeds of the Brahmins became Hindus, while others who resisted became panchammas or remained Buddhists.

While maintaining their separate identity, the Dalits supported the Non-Brahmin movement (NBM) for a number of reasons: a common desire to challenge the Brahmins who as a dominant group in Tamil society subjugated them, and a common identity of 'Dravidian' based upon region, language, and the historical past, which, rather than caste, were the defining categories of the period. Third, both the non-Brahmins and Dalits—until at least the 1930s—were not attracted towards the Indian National Congress (INC) or the National Movement, which they identified with brahminical Hinduism, Gandhian viewpoint on caste, and northern domination. Despite these contradictions, the depressed classes remained a significant plank of non-Brahminism. But it could not succeed in integrating them into their fold, as the depressed classes did not trust the non-Brahmins who subjected them to indignities and the ideological orientation of the NBM was not unambiguously anti-feudal in character (Irschick 1969).

Distinct phases are visible in the development of an Adi-Dravid ideology and identity. In the early nineteenth century, under the leadership of M.C. Rajah, the Adi-Dravids formed the Depressed Classes Federation. It led movements based on the principle of equality using non-violent forms and entered politics.

The issues raised were temple entry, free movement on roads, in post offices, banning caste discriminatory practices, and abolishing untouchability—a good example being the breast cloth controversy among Nadar women (Hardgrave 1969). In the 1930s, the Self-Respect Movement (SRM) led by Ramaswami Naicker, also called 'Periyar' (great leader), created a radical political and cultural identity that functioned at a number of levels: as a broad-based forum for expression of non-Brahmin concerns, as a popular exponent of a radical philosophy of rights, and liberation of the Adi-Dravids, as a militant pressure group, etc. It included militant campaigns against untouchability, encouraging inter-caste marriages, upholding the right to enter temples, denouncing child marriage and the laws of Manu as 'inhuman', and running a number of Tamil journals which appealed to the Adi-Dravids (Ibid.). Due to these developments, the Adi-Dravids in Madras Presidency were socially more politicized than in the northern plains.

An important development in the post-Independence period has been the attempt to create an 'independent Dalit identity' in Tamil Nadu following the questioning of Dravidian ideology/identity since the mid-1980s. The Dravidian ideology of the colonial period was stridently anti-Brahmin, but contained within itself the seeds of separation between the 'clean' non-Brahmin groups and the Dalits. It never challenged the structural hierarchy except in symbolic ways—today non-Brahmins are in power, but Brahminism remains. A close examination reveals that it was a philosophical-historical construct by scholars of the Saiva Siddhanta School such as Maraimalai Adigal, meant to provide a new identity to the *Vellala*s vis-à-vis the Brahmins, and offered little to the *Sudra* and *Ati-Sudra* masses. Adigal, using a Western Enlightenment framework, in his writings traced the domination of the Brahmins to the invasion of the 'uncivilized' Aryans, who destroyed Saivism, the religion of the Vellalas who were the original rulers of the Tamil country (Pandian 1994b). In short, Adigal removed the Brahmin from the high pinnacle in Tamil society and placed the Vellalas there instead, while leaving the rest of the societal levels as they were—at the most exhibiting paternalism towards the lower orders. This philosophy created contradictions and even conflict with the SRM which was more inclusive of the lower orders. Throughout the 1930s, a polemical war of pamphlets and public functions took place between the two sides (Ibid.).

Rapid increase in democratic consciousness since the mid-1980s among Dalits has led to a critical re-examination and rejection of the Dravidian identity constructed in the colonial period. In politics, two lower caste groups renounced Dravidian ideology: the *Vanniyars* or lower backwards who formed a separate movement/party, the (PMK) (Muthu Kumar 1994) and the emergence of Dalit organizations, some of which have come together to form Dalit parties. These developments are based on the sentiment that the non-Brahmin movement and rule has considerably weakened the status of the Brahmins, and strength-ened the position of the non-Brahmins, without dra-matically improving that of the untouchables (Pandian 1987). Dalit leaders point out that reservations for the Backward Classes (BCs) have increased considerably with successive governments increasing quotas. The Dravida Munnetra Kazhagam (DMK) in 1989 gave the Most Backward Classes (MBCs) 20 per cent of the total reservations while it increased reservations for Scheduled Castes/Scheduled Tribes (SC/ST) from 16 per cent to 18 per cent. Land alienation is also a fraught issue as *thevars* have bought up Dalit lands, and the latter are also no longer prepared to endure slavery.

Moreover, while there has been considerable educational and economic empowerment of Dalits in Tamil Nadu, this has not been matched by equal treatment on the part of the backward classes. The long anti-Brahmin movement has not brought a change in the thinking of the upper/middle castes. Social ostracism being deeply rooted in the Hindu psyche, Dalits have suffered from increasing social exclusion and isolation. Even conversion to Islam, Christianity, or Buddhism does not remove the stigma of untouchability.

In the villages, the Dalits are still segregated and face routine insults such as being served tea in different glasses at tea stalls, their marriage processions not being allowed through the main streets and being excluded from temple rituals. Another important reason has been the de-radicalization of the Dravidian ideology. Untouchability, which was a central issue in the 1930s, has lost its centrality. The communists are the only group who press for its abolition, but with little external support. The Brahmins have been ideologically re-incorporated into the Tamil community on the basis of regional and linguistic identity. The DMK renounced its anti-Brahmin stand and actively canvassed for the support of Brahmins in the 1967 elections and during subsequent elections. The All India Anna Dravida Munnetra Kazhagam (AIADMK) established the TN Brahmin Association (TAMBRAS) appointing Jayalalithaa, a Brahmin, as propaganda secretary and later as Chief Minister, giving tickets to a large number of Brahmins in the Assembly elections, representation in the Cabinet, temple renovation, and an alliance with the Bharatiya Janata Party (BJP) (Pai 2000).

However, no Dalit identity has emerged, that has been able to bring together various sub-castes among which there are major differences and competition. An integrated economic, cultural, and ideological alternative to upper and middle caste hegemony has yet to emerge. The change which has taken place is the rise of Dalit organizations in the southern districts following caste riots in these districts. However, these organizations became institutionalized into Dalit parties, an aspect, that is, dealt with in Chapter 3.

Gandhian

In contrast to the Tamil speaking areas of the Madras Presidency, a seminal feature of the Hindi heartland in the colonial period, continuing into the early years of independence, was the delayed development of Dalit consciousness among the large mass of untouchables (Pai 2002). This region did not experience any large-scale or sustained Dalit movement until very late in the colonial period, its impact in terms of mobilization upon the masses of the depressed classes was limited, and it came too late to have a transformative impact on society. Rather a series of small, widely separated, and weak movements took place which did not coalesce into one large movement, as in the Bombay presidency, until very late in the colonial period (Ibid.). There was little economic development apart from commercialization of agriculture, leather, and few other industries in western Uttar Pradesh and parts of Punjab, which otherwise could have played a catalytic role in breaking down the oppressive *Jajmani* village structure (Jurgensmeyer 1988; Wiser and Wiser 2001). Lack of cultural or political movements in the region meant the absence of any widespread anti-caste ideology and the passive acceptance of the unequal social and political system.

The ideological strand of Gandhism emerged in the 1920s from the thinking of Gandhi on the Hindu caste hierarchy, inter-caste relationships, method of caste reform, and the future role of the depressed classes in India. Importantly, it shaped the position of the INC during the national movement on the caste question. Gandhi believed in the *varna ashram dharma* and felt it was possible to continue the traditional concept of a varna system, but cleansed of untouchability, and in which the unclean work of the untouchables or 'Harijans' (literally children of God) would be made 'honourable'. Under Gandhi, from the 1920s onwards, the Congress adopted the social policy of *Harijan uddhar* or uplift and amelioration, rather than anti-caste mobilization.

The Gandhian ideology has been described as close to the orthodox or conservative tradition of social justice (Guru 2010: 362). Based on notions of purity–pollution, it gave hegemonic power to the twice-born castes, no choice for the untouchables to develop a 'technology' of the self and only 'relative worth', instead of 'comparative worth', thereby avoiding confrontation with other superior notions of worth (Ibid.). Also, there was violation of the traditional principle of co-responsibility, which makes it morally imperative on the part of members of the dominant sections to

13

own up to the problematic past which was created and handed down to them by their ancestors (Ibid. 366). In economic terms, this translated into the principle of 'trusteeship', that is, the rich being trustees on behalf of the poor, whom they were duty-bound to help. The Gandhian ideology tried to bring a change of heart within the upper castes by arousing their sympathy for the conditions of the Dalits.

Even before the advent of Gandhi, the early Congress leadership was passive to the need for ameliorating the conditions of the depressed classes. (Gupta 1985: 158) Congress leaders such as Tilak separated the social and political question, arguing that attaining independence was their goal, social issues such as caste-based inequalities could be resolved at a later stage. It was the colonial state that the depressed classes petitioned for help to improve their socio-economic conditions (Ibid.: 118). It was only 1909 onwards, when demands were raised for separate electorates, that the Congress leaders, realizing the need to support the depressed classes, changed their attitude somewhat. During the 28 months when the Congress was in power in the United Provinces during the 1930s, it established a Harijan Sewak Sangh and set aside Rs 3 lakh annually in the provincial budget for the education of the depressed classes, scholarships, stipends, and admitted depressed classes to teacher training schools in a bid to increase literacy among them. Leather industries were encouraged and efforts were made to stop untouchability and the practice of begging. This model of Harijan uddhar (uplift) once established, continued into the post-Independence period and created an unfavourable climate for the emergence of a movement from below (Pai 2002).

This ideology particularly affected the pattern of mobilization by the Congress in the northern plains during the national movement, especially where the lower castes were concerned. During the Kisan Sabha agitations of 1920–1 (Crawley 1971: 95) in the United Provinces and the Civil Disobedience and rent campaigns in 1930–1, low caste tenants and labourers participated in large numbers and threw up Pasi Madari, a low caste leader. The Congress leaders under Gandhi recognized the political importance of mass mobilization of the peasantry by supporting their grievances as part of the struggle. However, once the movements acquired a degree of autonomy and incorporated some of the basic contradictions of Indian society—such as the unequal caste/class hierarchy—

the leadership made a conscious effort to separate the political and social issues and called off the movement (Pandey 1978: 206).

Following Independence, the Gandhian ideology was adopted by the Congress party and remained the basis of programmes for SCs, particularly in the Nehruvian period. A recent study, using oral history and political talk with the older generations, describes the bond between the SCs and the Congress, their remembrances and feelings about the Nehruvian period (Narayan 2011). While the older persons knew little about Ambedkar, they were familiar with the ideas of Gandhi and Nehru. They recalled a mix of aspirations and hopes of emancipation from untouchability, inequality, and improvement in economic status (Ibid.: 19). They remembered Gandhi as a person who used to eat and drink with untouchables and treated them as equals; some had vivid memories about Nehru's campaigns in Phoolpur, the constituency from where he contested every election after Independence. For others, he was a 'mythical figure' and 'one of our own' who would provide freedom from caste oppression and feudal domination (Ibid.).

However, there were ambivalences and ambiguities among the older Dalits about the Nehruvian period. While they agreed that their conditions were improving, they were disappointed at the pace of change. The 1960s witnessed a shift from the identity of Harijan to Scheduled Caste and the brief success of the Republican Party of India (RPI). A feeling of disenchantment began with the Congress, though it continued to be the party supported by a majority of SCs in the country till the late 1980s, when it was gradually replaced by movements and parties based on the ideas of Ambedkar.

Ambedkarite and Post–Ambedkarite

Disillusionment with the Congress and its decline triggered rising interest in Ambedkarite ideology among SCs in the Hindi heartland, providing room in the 1980s for a new, post-Ambedkar Dalit leadership, that has built movements and parties based on sociocultural and political mobilization. Ambedkarite ideology, which has now spread in large parts of India, is the product of the writings and speeches of Dr Bhimrao

Ambedkar who emerged as an important leader of the depressed classes, but more particularly of the *Mahars* in the Bombay presidency (Gore 1993). He was a product of western India, where significant social reform movements had created notions of equality, leading to considerable ferment during the nineteenth century due to leaders such as Jyotiba Phule (O'Hanlon 1985). In sharp contrast to Gandhi, Ambedkar in his writings systematically constructed a philosophy of protest against caste-based oppression which provided legitimacy to the Mahar movement, and put the social question squarely at the centre of his thought (Gore 1993).

Ambedkar interrogated the caste system and Brahminical notions of justice, which makes his ideas close to the heterodox tradition of social justice (Guru 2010: 362). With twin adversaries to confront—colonial power and oppressive local power structures—the heterodox notion of social justice sought a nationalist and social resolution of justice. Ambedkar argued that the untouchables might belong to the same religion as the caste Hindus, but were not part of the same *samaj* (society) and formed a separate historically exploited social group, based on a religious philosophy of inequality found in the *Manusmriti*. He equated the philosophy of Brahminism with Hinduism as one of graded inequality which was inflexible. Based on his writings, Ambedkar put forward a threefold path for the depressed classes which formed the core of his ideology and legacy: educate, agitate, and organize.

By means of protest movements, Ambedkar from the mid-1920s onwards, tried to reform Hinduism through acts such as burning of the Manusmriti, the Chowdar tank protest, temple entry, and annual Mahar conferences to create awareness and assert the rights of the untouchables. In the 1930s, he realized that anti-caste movements could not change the Hindu social hierarchy and moved to political action. Thus in contrast to Gandhian mobilization in the Hindi heartland, the Mahars under the leadership of Ambedkar used both protest movements and political means consistently in their attempt to ameliorate social conditions and acquire political skills favourable to their assimilation into the broader mainstream (Zelliot 1979: 29). Zelliot, contrasting the position of Gandhi and Ambedkar on the caste question, finds the former leaning towards accommodation and the latter confrontationist (Ibid.). These differing positions arguably helped shape different identities among the depressed class communities in northern and western India with varying levels of consciousness and varied consequences for Dalit politics in independent India. Ambedkar also felt the Mahars could be a third force in the confrontation between the Hindus and the Muslims in the colonial period and also depend on the British to help them. Finally, when he found that untouchables could not find an equal status within Hinduism, he held that the Mahars could 'kick away the worthless Hindu identity' and convert to a different religion, an idea that he was considering from the late 1920s itself (Ibid.).

In the early post-Independence period, two Ambedkarite movements/parties emerged—the RPI in 1957 and the Dalit Panthers in 1972. The former was a party designed by Ambedkar prior to his death and proved to be a flash phenomenon, winning few seats in the mid-1960s—a period of Congress weakness—in states such as Uttar Pradesh (UP) and Maharashtra, and then declined. The latter failed to ignite a mass movement, but left a rich legacy of Dalit *sahitya* (literature) which left its mark on Maharashtrian society. Both political parties are discussed in Chapter 3. By the mid-1980s, democratization and rising socio-political consciousness among the SCs led to the emergence of a strong wave of Dalit assertion based on Ambedkarite ideology in the Hindi heartland. Dalit intellectuals of the pre-Independence era had been linked to many different ideologies and organizations and were active in the fight for emancipation as writers, thinkers, and social reformers. Following the decline of Gandhian ideology, the Ambedkarite ideology spread to many states.

The post-Ambedkarite ideology is best understood by examining the writings of Kanshi Ram, the ideologue of the BSP. The BSP formed in 1984, claims to be an Ambedkarite movement-turned-party. A fundamental tenet of his ideology is that the basic divide in India is not class-based, but caste-based—the *Sawarna*s (upper castes) who on the basis of birth have occupied a privileged socio-economic and political position as the ruling class, and the low caste Sudra and Ati-Sudras or Dalits who have remained poor and occupied a menial social position. The latter form the *moolnivasi* (original inhabitants) who were conquered by the Aryans and reduced to untouchables, creating an unequal social order which has the sanction of religion and custom. According to Kanshi Ram, Hinduism

21

and Brahminism—which is part of Hinduism—is not a religion but a sociocultural ideology that has divided the majority into innumerable caste groups and prevented them from entering and achieving positions of power in all aspects of life, including politics. (Pai 2002).

The BSP began as a *Bahujan* movement, that is, constituting the majority of the downtrodden, and drawing upon the ideas of Jyotiba Phule. More important, it was an identity constructed to unite the backward and SCs, who as Kanshi Ram pointed out, together constitute more than 50 per cent of the population in UP. But the attempt to create a Bahujan Samaj failed by the early 1990s due to fundamental differences with the backwards. Subsequently, the BSP has described itself as a Dalit movement or party, whose aim is to provide self-respect, dignity, and empowerment to all sections of the ex-untouchables. The term Dalit more narrowly means caste discrimination, in comparison to the Dalit Panthers, which draws upon both Ambedkarism and Marxism to imbue the term with a class implication and attempts revolutionary transformation of society.

The ideology of the BSP is similar to the anti-Brahmin movements of southern and western India, but its anti–Brahminism is more political than cultural. According to Kanshi Ram, one of Ambedkar's basic tenets was that 'political power is the key by which any lock (obstacle) can be opened'. Capture of state power is needed since it is under the control of *manu-vadi* leaders. Once captured it is the instrument through which social justice for Dalits, different from the sort promised by mainstream parties, can be attained. It is exclusive, that is, only for the Dalits because they have been the most exploited section of Indian society, and retributive, that is, it seeks to rectify 'historical wrongs' imposed on them by the upper caste Hindus, and tries to establish a new social and political order. The new social order can be achieved by using state power 'from above' for social engineering, that is, introducing developmental and welfare programmes for Dalit upliftment rather than a revolution based on mobilization and destruction of the existing unequal social order 'from below'. This has been criticized as a sponsored notion of justice which can lead to coopta-tion, in contrast to 'contestary' justice associated with subaltern contestations against the upper castes in civil society (Guru 2010). Although the BSP attempts total revolution, that is, destruction rather than reform of the Hindu social and political order, it is to take place not through social upheaval, but through the ballot box. Kanshi Ram visualized two stages: first capturing power through mobilization and electoral victory against the Brahmins, and in the second phase the revolution would penetrate deeper into society, transforming it (Pai 2002).

A major shift took place in the ideology of the BSP, in early twenty-first century, under the leadership of Mayawati. With the weakening of identity politics in the Hindi heartland, the BSP decided to transform itself from an avowedly Dalit party to a broader 'social rainbow coalition' or savarna party with a Dalit core, and to rethink its strategies of electoral mobilization in order to gain the support of the upper castes. Earlier, the BSP gave tickets to a large number of non-Dalits, but now it attempted to gain the support of the twice-born castes by approaching and mobilizing them directly (Pai 2007).

Consequently, in the electoral campaign for the 2007 Assembly elections, Brahmin *sammelan*s were held and Mayawati was greeted at rallies with Brahminical rituals such as the chanting of Vedic hymns, new symbols, and the blowing of conches, while Brahmin leaders of the party presented gifts to her (*The Hindu* 2005). A basic point that Mayawati put forward was that her party had never been against the upper-caste communities or the Hindu religion, but was opposed to caste oppression. Though the true mission was to build an egalitarian society free of caste divisions, the BSP had been misrepresented as an anti-upper-caste party (*The Hindu* 2005). Mayawati argued that Dalits and Brahmins could together rule the state and pointed out that Ambedkar 'not only accepted a Brahmin surname given by a Brahmin teacher but also married a Brahmin' (Ibid.).

Following the defeat of the BSP in the 2012 Assembly elections, it has been argued that a section of the *Chamar-Jatav*s, who traditionally formed the core social base of the BSP, unhappy with the ideology of *Sarvajan* did not vote for the party (Verma 2012). Some studies have held that Dalits were unhappy with the importance given by Mayawati to Brahmins who were given Cabinet posts and other economic benefits.

More importantly, in terms of ideology, both cultural and economic issues are significantly involved. Some sections feel that the adoption of such an ideology would dilute the Dalit identity of the party constructed through hard grass roots struggle, Others, who have waited long for the party to obtain a majority, are no longer satisfied with self-respect and dignity as in the past—they expected that the BSP as a ruling party would take urgent steps to improve the material conditions of Dalits in UP. For them the politics of symbolism through statues and memorials to Dalit icons no longer holds much appeal. These developments raise the fundamental issue of the ideology and future direction of the Dalit movement in UP.

★ ★ ★

Different ideological strands have developed within the Dalit movement due to the large size, and regional, and cultural diversity of the Indian subcontinent. This explains the uneven development of the Dalit movement across the country. As the following chapters will show, there is no all-India movement or party. Rather diverse identities and distinct forms of mobilization have developed in each region. An important reason for this diversity is timing—Dalit consciousness and related movements emerged much earlier in the colonial period in southern and western than in northern India, resulting in a distinct north–south divide. The lack of Dalit leaders in many areas was also a seminal reason for the late emergence of socio-political consciousness among Dalits. Leaders such as Ambedkar or Periyar were known mainly in their own regions until the late colonial period. Sub-caste differences—which are dealt with in detail in the next chapter—have also been important. In each region there is both competition as well as collaboration among them. Due to these reasons, it was only after almost three decades of independence and democratization that mobilization and movements emerged on a large scale in the Hindi heartland. Everywhere Dalits have common problems—the most important being untouchability and caste-based atrocities—as well as goals and aspirations, but the manner in which they have sought to address their problems and attain their goals have been different.

Our study has identified three major ideological strands: Gandhian, Dravidian, and Ambedkarite. While the Gandhian strand emerged in the Hindi heartland, its features can be found in other backward regions such as Orissa or Madhya Pradesh where Dalit consciousness remained low. There were few attempts by Dalit leaders to mobilize and challenge upper caste hegemony in a sustained manner. Associated with Nehruvian India, it lost importance following the decline of the Congress party in the 1980s, providing space for Ambedkarite movements/parties such as the BSP. In contrast, Dravidian ideology, supported by the Dalits and the non-Brahmin middle castes, emerged very early in the colonial period. Both wanted to challenge the hegemony of the Brahmin, also identified as Aryan, and therefore alien. Within the larger non-Brahmin movement, some Dalit movements were radical in nature.

However, since the 1980s, Dalits have moved closer to the Ambedkarite ideology. But, they have not been able to give up their Dravidian identity since it is also linked historically with language, culture, and region and thus no alternative independent Dalit identity has emerged. With the decline of Gandhian ideology, a process of ideological homogenization seems to have taken place (Narayan 2010: 84). It is the Ambedkarite ideology that has caught the imagination of the younger generation of Dalits across the country. While initially it became important in the Hindi heartland due to mobilization by leaders such as Kanshiram, it has now spread to southern India. The extensive spread of Ambedkarite thought at the grass roots—discussed in the next chapter—provides ample evidence of this fact.

2

Dalit Assertion at
the Grass Roots

In recent years, the Dalit challenge to upper caste
domination and oppression has taken two main forms:
mobilization through movements and political parties
and assertion at the grass roots. In the absence today
of large, organized Dalit movements, analysis of movements at the grass roots is important as it can break new
ground in our understanding of the history of contemporary politics of empowerment and change. Assertion
at the grass roots is not a product of the mobilizational
activities of Dalit movements or parties. Rather it is
a phenomenon that is much larger and deeper than,
and predates, the emergence of movements and
parties—and though in many cases it underlies the

construction of Dalit identity—it has an independent existence. Unlike Dalit movements and parties, it takes non-political forms involving multifaceted social and economic activities. At the same time, there is a complex relationship between assertion at the grass roots and Dalit movements and parties. While the former has been a gradual—and at times almost a subterranean process—the latter has given it greater strength with the process often receiving a fillip. Parties have also attempted to harness this force at the grass roots for electoral gains. However, the two have retained their distinct course; movements or parties have not been able to overshadow the activities taking place at the grass roots level. In fact, those involved in Dalit assertion at the grass roots since the 1980s have often been critical of, and antithetical to, the positions that movements and parties have taken.

Some parts of the country did witness lower caste consciousness and activism during the colonial period and the first few decades after independence. However, assertion at the grass roots is largely a post-Independence phenomenon. During the Nehruvian period, Dalits supported the Congress party in large parts of the country, particularly the Hindi heartland. Writing about this period in a recent study, Narayan points out that in Uttar Pradesh, the Dalits shared a special relationship with Nehru and had high expectations that he would release them from upper caste oppression (Narayan 2010). The memory of Nehru seems to have served a triple purpose to Dalits of this generation. First, it reminded them of their own aspirations of freedom from colonialism, the caste system, and other administrative oppressions. Second, it reinforced belief in a 'king' who would liberate them from poverty and bring development into the villages. Finally, it also cemented the belief that their liberator would be one of 'their own', who though not from their community, could begin the task of building a democratic and more egalitarian society in which they as yet, had little say or participation (Ibid.). However, a phase of disillusionment with the Congress party, began in the late Nehruvian period, which deepened by the 1970s. This set the stage for rising politicization, and it is from the 1980s onwards that Dalit assertion at the grass roots has become more visible, and is a 'qualitatively new phenomenon'.

Assertion over the last three decades has taken many forms—in this chapter three main aspects are discussed. Deeply unhappy with the failure of the state to protect the life and property of Dalits, improve their socio-economic conditions, and end the practice of untouchability—Dalits have constructed alternative ideologies such as Ambedkarization to create political consciousness, and based on it, social and cultural activities against oppression and domination. Second, grass roots assertion has enabled Dalits to challenge oppressive practices and atrocities by the locally dominant landowning upper and middle castes at the village level which has led to conflict and at times violence. Third, assertion at the grass roots has not created homogenization—rather it has led to fragmentation and divisions among Dalit sub-castes—leading to rivalry and conflict which has impacted upon politics. Examples are taken from three states—UP, Tamil Nadu, and Punjab—where grass roots activity is most visible and an attempt is made to understand the linkages and contributions of these often subterranean forms with more visible and mainstream Dalit politics. This exercise provides a backdrop to the study of Dalit political parties in the next chapter.

Assertion at the Grass roots:
Forms and Features

Ambedkarization

An important base for the growth of grass roots assertion in the Hindi heartland, particularly in Uttar
Pradesh, has been the process of Ambedkarization
(Singh 1998). The term refers to multifaceted activities emerging from the growth in the consciousness
among the Dalits, particularly the Chamar-Jatavs in
western Uttar Pradesh, about the life and teachings
of Ambedkar. Ambedkarization, it has been argued,
enhances consciousness of Dalit identity, low caste
status, and desire to improve it. It is a progressive
ideology that attacks the entire caste system and goes
much beyond what Dalit parties stand for. Since the
1980s, grass roots assertion has entered a period of
revolt, after many years of fragmentation and cooption
by the Congress. But this process since the 1980s is a
'second phase' (Ibid.) of an older grass roots process
in the region in the 1940s when the Chamar-Jatavs
of western Uttar Pradesh began to be attracted to the
writings and activities of Ambedkar (Jurgensmeyer
1988; Lynch 1969), and the mid-1960s, when the

34

Republican Party of India (RPI) was active (Duncan 1979; Singh 1998). The RPI was both a sociocultural movement and a party evident from its support to education and conversion to Buddhism. Districts such as Meerut, Allahabad, Lucknow, Agra, and Kanpur witnessed early Ambedkarite mobilization while other regions seem to have remained almost untouched until mobilization by the Bahujan Samaj Party (BSP).

Following the disappearance of the RPI, the process of Ambedkarization dwindled, but continued in Meerut district particularly at an individual level in which education and conversion to Buddhism seem to have played a key role (Singh 1998: 2616). Good examples are Amar Singh of village Nagla Hareru and Master Asha Ram of village Maithena Inder Singh close to Meerut city, who converted to Buddhism and, in their spare time, disseminated the ideas of Ambedkar by distributing his writings, discussing them, and stressing the need to discard the Hindu religion. A second generation of Dalits, which entered colleges and universities in the 1970s, was also conversant with the ideas of Ambedkar (though some left the village to seek jobs elsewhere). This generation had an impact upon the present third generation including the poorer and illiterate Dalits, who are extremely committed to the ideas of Ambedkar. Politicization and identity awareness is high among them and they actively protest against upper caste domination in both the sociocultural and political spheres (Singh 1998). The process of Ambedkarization is therefore the important thread that binds the period of the RPI with that of the BSP and helped in the formation of the latter (Pai 2002).

Dalit assertion in Meerut district at the grass roots has taken two major forms in recent years: use of socio-political and cultural symbols and establishment of Dalit organizations. The former is seen in many villages/towns where committees, schools, and libraries named after Ambedkar have been set up. His statues have been installed in many villages, his birthday is celebrated with great fervour—plays exposing upper castes oppression are staged, *prabhat pheri*s and processions to the accompaniment of songs and praise of Ambedkar are taken out. The participants in such processions exhort Dalits to read Dalit literature, not to compromise on dignity, use 'Jai Bhim' as a greeting instead of 'Ram Ram'. In recent years, there has also been a growth of Ambedkar schools, that is, private, unaided, and unrecognized schools in Meerut district—both in the district and in Meerut city—which have been set up by educated Dalits who feel that the government schools are inadequate and would like their children to compete with upper caste children in all walks of life. Ambedkarization has led Dalits to assert 'everyday forms of resistance' at the village level and has also led to a growing protest literature (Singh 1998).

In contrast, the establishment of Dalit organizations is an economic and political activity. Two kinds of Dalit organizations exist in western Uttar Pradesh and increasingly, elsewhere too (Pai 2000a). Caste panchayats or mahasabhas, exist in the villages surrounding Meerut city, organized by educated pradhans of villages with a large Dalit population, which provide a network able to mobilize against any incident of atrocity. They have elaborate rules regarding membership from different villages, leaders at various levels going up to a regional president and collection of funds. They hold regular meetings in panchayat bhawans, or the Ambedkar Schools found all over Meerut. Apart from these, Ambedkar Sudhhar Samitis exist in almost all villages to help solve daily problems of Dalits such as protection of Jatavs from atrocities (Ibid.).

The second type of Dalit assertion in Meerut City consists of modern voluntary—and in some cases—registered associations of Dalits such as the Samyukta Dalit Morcha, Rashtriya Soshit Morcha, etc. (Pai 2003). These associations were formed by educated Dalit leaders such as lawyers or teachers. The purpose of these associations, formed in the early 1990s, was to protect the interests of Dalits which were increasingly being perceived as being neglected by the state. They helped Dalits gain education, employment, enabled access to legal aid, provided assistance in dealing with the police and in setting up businesses, etc. These associations were not set up by the BSP, nor are they its branches, but there is overlapping membership and many associations do campaign for the BSP during elections. Leaders of these organizations were very critical of the BSP when it converted from a movement to a party, and some allied with the BJP, an upper caste party in 1995. However, they argue that they vote for the BSP as they have no other option. Thus the relationship between the grass roots movements and Dalit parties is ambivalent, critical at some times supportive during others (Ibid.).

A recent study on Dalit organizations in Kanpur city, a historic Ambedkarite stronghold, examines the intricate relationship that evolved during the first decade of the twenty-first century between non-political grass roots organizations and the BSP (Jaoul 2007). It argues that these two poles represent different, and sometimes conflicting, strategies that have coexisted historically and relied on each other to create the specificity of the Dalit movement in the state. Non-political organizations such as the Bharatiya Dalit Panthers in Kanpur have become intermediaries between the Dalits and the local administration. Their activists have been able to pressurize the local administration from below while the BSP governments implemented their political agenda from above. Most Dalits in the city agree with the non-political Ambedkarite critique of the BSP's evolution, but at the same time are strongly committed to Mayawati, who they feel has been able to deliver the goods (Ibid.).

In Tamil Nadu, Ambedkarization is a recent though significant phenomenon. Dalit mobilization at the grass roots is much older than in many other states, beginning early in the colonial period. The Dalits supported the non–Brahmin movement, and in the immediate post-Independence period, the Dravidian parties. Until the 1980s, Ambedkar was not well known in the state, and Periyar was a major icon. But over the last two decades, the Dalits have moved away from the Dravidian parties and attempted autonomous mobilization, (Pandian 2000) with Ambedkar identified as the symbol of assertion which has brought the state closer to the Hindi heartland.

Two phases can be identified. The first was in the 1980s when Dalits used conversion as a form of protest because they were unhappy with the asymmetry between their considerably improved material conditions and unequal social status accorded to them by the backward castes. This arose from their new-found separate identity of Dravidianism. The Dalits argued that despite supporting the Dravidian parties, they had not been well treated or protected by these parties when in power. About 2,600 Dalits in the southern districts of Tirunelveli, Ramananthapuram, and Madurai converted to Islam between February and September 1981. This included Meenakshipuram, a prosperous village in which the Dalits were educated and in good government and private jobs. This resulted in violence between them and the middle castes in many places.

A second phase began in the 1990s when Ambedkarization began across the state. Though in the first three decades of independence Ambedkar was not well known, in this phase statues, posters and nameplates bearing his image have proliferated and halls schools and colleges are named after him (Delige 1977; Gorringe 2005). The attempt at the grass roots has been to move away from the Dravidian identity and develop an independent Dalit identity. This phase saw great social turbulence in the southern districts particularly in the late 1990s in places such as Chidambaranar, Nellai Kattabormman, and Kamarajar leading to the formation of Dalit organizations. These included organizations such as Devendrakula Vellalar Sangam led by John Pandian, an aggressive speaker who incited violence between the Dalits and the Thevars in many places leading in some cases to riots—the Devendrakula Vellalar Federation formed in 1995, by well-known cardiologist Dr Krishnasamy, which later became a political party—the Puthiya Tamilagam (PT) and the Thiyagi Immanuel Peravai formed by P. Chandrabose in 1988 named after the famous Pallan youth icon and leader Immanuel Sekaran (Manikumar 1997: 2242). North Tamil Nadu also experienced autonomous mobilization by the Parayars but it was not as well organized as in the south. It gave rise to simmering conflict between the Parayars and the upper caste Udayars, leading to open conflict during the Ambedkar centenary celebrations during which the local Parayar youth formed an organization named the Kodunkaal Ambedkar Mantram. This eventually led to greater confrontation, violence, and a case in the Madras High Court creating more animosity (Pandian 2000: 10).

The struggle by Dalits for Panchamma lands or Depressed Class lands granted to them by the colonial rulers and the Indian state after Independence has been important at the grass roots. According to the law, Panchamma or Depressed Class land issued under a special standing order—now called revenue standing order—cannot be sold to a non-Dalit. However, much of this land has been encroached upon by middle caste landowners, often with the connivance of district officials. This has led to many clashes, such as the Karanai incident in 1995, where over 650 acres were seized by middle castes and the Dalits installed a statue of Ambedkar to reassert their rights over the land. The middle castes pulled down and disfigured the statue which led to violent clashes across the district and police firing (Moses 1995: 247). Many Non-governmental Organizations (NGOs) have tried to help Dalits to regain control over such lands. These include the Social Action Movement (SAM) formed in 1994 by the Save Panchamma Land Committee with representatives from various villages (Ibid.: 248). Dalits who attained prosperity through education and government jobs or money repatriated from the Gulf, and tried to buy land in their own villages in the 1990s, had to face violent resistance (Manikumar 1997).

Another important aspect that affects grass roots activities is the relationship between the Dalit movement and the state. A widely held perception is that the State in Tamil Nadu, through its police forces and courts, is biased against the Dalits and does not provide them with justice or intervene to help them when they are being killed (Thirumavalvaan 2003). Rather than addressing the basic issue of unequal social power at the local level, the response of the state in most cases is to provide economic compensation to Dalits such as giving them a milk cooperative, building or repairing houses, bore wells, roads, etc. (Pandian 2000). The Civil Rights Act or the Atrocities Act is not used on most occasions and the record of convictions secured under it is very dismal. The state government is also reluctant to accord recognition to the Dalit in the public realm through the renaming roads or public facilities after Dalit icons. This has been true of both the Dravida Munnetra Kazhagam (DMK) and the All India Anna Dravida Munnetra Kazhagam (AIADMK). An off-shoot of the rise in social tension has been an increase in Dalit consciousness at the grass roots which in turn has led to further violence.

Other sources of discrimination still exist in many villages which affect relationships between Dalits and backwards: wells and temples are still out of bounds for Dalits, separate place of worship and deities exist; municipal schools cater largely to Dalits since middle castes send their children to private schools; though steel tumblers have replaced coconut shells Dalits continue to be served separately in tea stalls; they are not allowed to use cement benches at bus stops and made to sit on the floor in panchayat offices despite being elected representatives. Minimum wages are not implemented by landlords and the worst jobs are reserved for

Dalits—but this is in areas where Dalits are not educationally empowered. Another reason responsible for increased discrimination against Dalits is the attempt made in the 1990s to unite all the various Thevar sub-castes. This has made them aggressive, which is seen in the installation of large number of statues of their leaders. The breaking or defilement of such statues by Dalits led to clashes. Consequently, social relationships have broken down in the state especially in the southern districts. Thus, unlike in Uttar Pradesh where grass roots activities have led to increased understanding of the writings of Ambedkar and political empowerment under the BSP, in Tamil Nadu it has created tremendous competition and day-to-day violence against Dalits by middle castes such as the Thevars and Gounders.

An important product of these grass roots struggles has been the emergence of vibrant Dalit literature arising out of the upsurge from below in the state. It portrays a new feeling of confidence and fresh thinking on questions of nation, democracy, citizenship, and development. A recent study points to the sociology of Dalit intellectual formations and literature as having an organic link with grass roots social reality and political mobilization. The writers have published their work in small magazines which they have produced with their own meagre resources rather than in mainstream vernacular publishing (Satyanarayana and Tharu 2011). This shows that Dalit assertion has been autonomous both in form and content and this dialectical relationship between these two aspects is reflected in the spirit of their writings (Srinivasulu 2011: 30). However, some scholars have argued that while these writings have questioned both past classical writings as reproducing upper caste norms and present day inequalities, they have been silent about gender or sub-caste divisions due to which there is oppression within the Dalit community that does not allow the emergence of a singular Dalit identity (Anandhi 2011: 27).

In Punjab the Dera movement, which is sweeping through the grass roots, is comparable to the process of Ambedkarization among the Chamars in Uttar Pradesh and has similar strengths. Due to democratization, increased literacy and rising prosperity, grass roots movements have introduced tremendous social change leading to dissociation, distancing, and autonomy (Jhodka 2010). Dalits have dissociated themselves from traditional occupations, considered demeaning, such as lifting or skinning dead cattle and scavenging; less than 5 per cent are associated with such tasks in the present day. Instead they have entered into large scale and highly profitable commercial relations in these very tasks with the locally dominant castes at the panchayat and village level. Dalits have found ways of dealing with separation or exclusion by the upper and middle castes: they have built their own autonomous village settlements, Gurudwaras, cremation grounds, schools and, marriage halls with their own funds. In democratic politics also due to the breakdown of the hierarchical power structure of the village community and the jajmani system, in which feudal upper/middle caste landlords exercised control over the land and labour of the lower castes, Dalits feel free to vote according to their own choice. Thus, caste is alive but has assumed new forms creating strong divisions at the grass roots.

The root of these changes at the grassroot level in the Punjab can be traced to the colonial period, though its direction and impact is rather different from Uttar Pradesh and Tamil Nadu. The Ad-Dharm movement beginning in the 1920s, under the leadership of Mangoo Ram—a leader originally from the Arya Samaj in Jalandhar—attempted to create an alternative religion for the Chamars of the Doaba region, drawing upon both the tenets of Sikhism and Islam (Jurgensmeyer 1988). The movement did not throw up a religion but it succeeded in providing a new identity, self-confidence and a religious worldview which would distinguish the Chamars from the Hindus. Described as Sikhism for the lower castes, Ad-Dharm adopted the form of *Satsang* or community worship using the writings of Ravi Dass, a lower caste saint. Nearly 80 per cent of the lower caste population of Jalandhar and Hoshiarpur districts renamed themselves as Ad-Dharmis in the British census of 1931 and attained a more respectable stature compared to other sections of the scheduled castes in Punjab. With a rise in interest in the work of Ambedkar in the 1930s, the Ad-Dharm movement declined but it had already had an impact on the Chamars (Ibid.). The Ad-Dharmis have attempted to mobilize all the lower castes through movements such as the Scheduled Caste Federation (SCF) in the 1940s, and later through the RPI and the BSP, though these parties have not been as strong as in Uttar Pradesh.

After independence, the Chamars of the Doaba, under the Ravi Dass Mandal formed in 1946, attempted to develop an autonomous Dalit consciousness and social and religious resources at the grass roots (Jodhka and Kumar 2010). It espoused a 'middle path' of social mobility for the Dalits without sacrificing their distinct identity. This was neither radical separatism advocated by the conversion model of Ambedkar nor the path of assimilation advocated by the Arya Samaj or the Khalsa Diwan, that is, the Hindu or Sikh model (Ibid.). Over 250 Ravi Dass Deras—some of which are very prosperous and influential—have been built in the Punjab. A number of *sant*s (saints) who are considered leaders of the community are active at the grass roots. The most important Dera today is located in the village of Ballan, about 10 kms from Jalandhar town, locally called the Dera Sachkhand Ballan. Originally set up in the early twentieth century by Sant Pipal Dass, it has now become a centre of Dalit activity. Studies indicate that all those who visit it are mainly from the Chamar/Ad-Dharm caste, and among whom it promotes a sense of pride, empowerment, and autonomy. The Dera has set up schools, hospitals, and charitable institutions. As the Chamars in many villages are not allowed into Gurudwaras or temples, the Dera provides them a religious place and also looks after their social and economic needs. Since the Dera Sachkhand

Ballan has become the epicentre of social protest and Dalit political activity in the Punjab, leaders, writers, and intellectuals of the community often meet and discuss emerging political and cultural challenges facing the Ravi Dass community. Kanshi Ram, who was born into a Ravidasi family, was a frequent visitor to the Dera to discuss strategies with other leaders of the community in order to make Dalit policies more effective.

The phenomenon of Ambedkarization is not limited to the examples given above but has been spreading, though in different forms, to various regions in the country. West Bengal, a state popularly associated with class politics due to the rule by the Left parties for a long period of time, has in recent years witnessed politicization and assertion in districts such as Nadia, Burdwan, Birbhum, and Purulia which have a large number of Dalits (Bhattacharyya 2003). The rise of Dalit literature or *Matua Sahitya* and the establishment of Dalit writers associations and magazines points to much change at the grass roots (Byapari 2009; Ganguly-Scrase 2001). Similar developments have been noted in Orissa, a state which did not experience any large movements in the post-Independence movement. In recent years, the state has experienced movements in the coastal region which has traditionally been a region of upper caste domination. A study has pointed to temple entry movements by Dalits in districts such as Kendrapara which have led to violent reaction (Malik 2011).

Conflict at the Grass Roots:
Dalits versus the Backwards

Identity assertion has led to increased discrimination and violence at the grass roots against Scheduled Castes (SCs) by the upper and middle castes in many parts of the country, particularly in the rural areas. While this has been a pervasive feature from the colonial period, some new features have characterized crimes against SCs since the late 1970s. First, the number of caste-based crimes against SCs increased sharply in the 1980s and 1990s. Second, discrimination based on various forms of ritual untouchability has been largely replaced by caste atrocities such as rape, not allowing SCs to cast their votes, burning of houses, parading naked women in village streets, and breaking or removing Ambedkar statues. Third, most of these crimes are perpetrated by the traditionally dominant, landowning middle or backward castes such as the Jats, Gujjars, and Yadavs in the Hindi heartland, and Thevars and Gounders in Tamil Nadu who today constitute the direct oppressors of the SCs and try to humiliate and suppress attempts by them to improve their social and economic conditions. Finally, a significant reason for atrocities has been the breaking and defilement of Ambedkar statues, which is extremely humiliating for the SCs. The SCs and Scheduled Tribes (STs) (Prevention of Atrocities) Act 1989 and the (Prevention of Atrocities) Rules 1995, has not solved the problem and has only led to greater confrontation. Correspondingly, relations with the upper and middle castes range from subservience and repression in remote and poorer areas to militancy and tolerance in better-off regions. This does not mean that untouchability, and therefore atrocities arising from socio-cultural factors, have disappeared. It is prevalent in various forms: no access to temples, drinking water sources, tea stalls and hotels, denial of services of barbers and washermen, denying participation in social ceremonies, sitting in chaupals, using cremation grounds, etc. A study on untouchability by Action Aid across a number of states had documented such exclusion (Shah *et al.* 2006).

Tamil Nadu provides the best example of high levels of violence and escalating conflict, since the 1990s, between the backward castes and the Dalits (Gorringe 2005; Pandian 2000; Parthasarthi 2011). The reasons lie in the asymmetrical power relationships that have emerged in villages as Dalits, particularly the Devendars, have advanced by obtaining degrees and good jobs while the Thevars and other backward groups have remained small and marginal farmers. The former demand equal honour at temple festivals and other village rituals, which the Thevars are reluctant to accord, as it would challenge their traditional position. It is the educated Dalit youth that is involved in much of the violent clashes. A good example is Vadananthampati, a village in southern Tamil Nadu, which had about 300 Dalit graduates who according to a study were 'combustible material' as they were not prepared to put up with oppression (Manikumar 1997: 2243). Consequently, the middle castes specially the Thevars, could no longer exercise ideological hegemony over the former and needed to use violence to affirm their authority (Pandian 2000:1). The Thevars, who still carry the pride and image of a martial community which was once supposed to have ruled

Tamil Nadu, feel that their marginalization is due to too many privileges accorded to the Dalits by the state in the form of concessions, reservations, land, etc. This sentiment was exploited during the 1990s, particularly by the AIAMDK, who supported the Thevars to gain their political support. This has encouraged the Thevars to take action against the Dalits.

In the southern districts, the conflict is between the backward caste Thevars and the Pallars (who have now renamed themselves as the Devendars) and in the northern districts between the most backward caste Vanniyars and the Parayars. Violence has existed in both areas since the colonial period. There are many examples of this such as Ramnad in 1957, Kilvenmani in 1969, and later Villupuram, Pennadam, Seekkanankuppam (where upper caste landlords attacked the Dalits), Kodiyankulam in 1996, Bodi in 1989, Naarai Kinaru in 1994, and the terrible Thevar–Dalit clashes in April–May 1997. What is significant is the changing characteristics of this violence in recent years. First, the time taken by the state to reestablish peace has been progressively increasing from five days in the early years of independence to nine months in 1985–6. Second, while earlier it was mostly Dalits who lost their lives, now they fight back, and on both sides there is loss of life and property. Third, caste conflicts are no longer local, but quickly spread over to a large area (Pandian 2000). A fourth feature is the manner in which the police deal with clashes between the Dalits and the Thevars and other backward middle castes. A study of the incident of the killing of six Dalits in police firing in Paramkudi in September 2011 when they were celebrating the 54th memorial day of Immanuel Sekaran, points to the continuing complicity between the dominant castes, political parties—particularly the AIADMK—and state institutions (Parathasarthi 2011: 14). The study argues that the Paramkudi violence was not the only one; police in the region are notorious for extorting, looting property, abusing women and children, beating men, and building false cases (Ibid.). These features explain the rising Dalit assertion at the grass roots in the state. A similar situation is seen in northern Tamil Nadu where the conflict is between the Vanniyars and Parayars. Here, though it is only a small section of the Vanniyars who have improved their status in comparison with the latter, leading to considerable social jealousy.

Much of grass roots violence is witnessed in the panchayats over issues of reservation (Pai 2006). Between
1999 to 2002, the reserved panchayat constituencies of
Pappapatti, Keeripatti, and Nattarmangalam in Madurai
district and Kottakatchiyendal in Virundhnagar district
had 10 announcements of elections. However, no Dalit
could even file his/her nomination papers in 9 out of
the 10. The Thevars in these village panchayats issued
a decree that any Dalit who dared to do so would
be killed. The elections were held under tight government security on October 28, but still saw much
violence. But in some villages, no nominations were
filed by Dalits and allegations were made of panchayat
posts being auctioned among the upper castes who
went on to make the de facto decisions in the panchayat instead of the elected Dalits. Thirumaavalvan
whose political party, the Dalit Panthers of India, has
often attempted to help the Dalits in Madurai district points out that such incidents have taken place
during the rule of both Dravidian parties: the DMK
and the AIADMK (Thirumaavalvan 2003). While
such incidents are due to continuation of untouchability, they are also due to the attempt to shift the

power equations from the upper to the lower castes or classes.

However, some recent accounts argue that two changes have taken place in the state. First, the stark violence such as riots and murders in the late 1990s has declined as Dalits have fought back in kind or in court. Second, the new forms of untouchability and caste violence have brought everyday repression into the open, in a way it had not earlier. It has pitted the intermediate castes and Dalits against each other everywhere and indicated that it is because of the former's desire to demonstrate that they are of higher status than their victims (Rajangam 2011).

Fragmentation: Conflict among Dalit Sub-castes

However, Dalit assertion at the grass roots has not created homogenization within the Dalit community. It has brought a realization of difference with the 'other'—the caste Hindu—but remains internally fragmented with both competition and collaboration among sub-castes. Two features of the caste system have also played a role. First, the existence of a hierarchy below the line of pollution which divides sub-castes some of whom do not inter-dine or inter-marry. Second, in every region there is one sub-caste which is numerically preponderant and dominant such as the Chamars in Uttar Pradesh, Mahars in Maharashtra, and the Vankars in Gujarat. The pattern of social and political change, since the colonial period, in which some sub-castes have benefitted more than others, has also been equally responsible. The dominant sub-castes everywhere, typically, are better educated and have made use of protective discrimination to gain jobs and other facilities, own land and have formed the vanguard of all movements including those at the grass roots. In the political arena, due to varying levels of politiciza-tion, there is space for fragmentation among Dalits, with the risk of Dalits being co-opted in a Hindutva project designed to communalize Dalit identity. The constant attempts of the BJP at 'saffronizing' the Dalits or carrying out 'social engineering' through grass roots mobilization, to bring them within the Hindutva fold in the Hindu heartland, are well documented (Jaffrelot 2003).

A good example of sub-caste rivalry is the socio-political division at the grass roots between the Chamars of western Uttar Pradesh, who have historically been the most prosperous and educated group, and other sub-castes, thus creating jealousy and hostility. In the 1931 census, out of the 21 per cent of the depressed classes in the population, Chamars made up 1.2 per cent, while the others were much less—Pasis 2.9 per cent, Dhobis 1.6 per cent, Bhangis 1.0 per cent, and the other sub-castes 2.8 per cent. In the colonial census, they managed to change their name from the demeaning Chamar to Jatav or Kureel, which they claim is a distinct group much higher than the other sub-castes. Prosperity gained from the leather industry, set up in parts of north India in the colonial period, enabled them to enter politics thus giving them an advance over the others (Lynch 1969). Capitalist economic development after independence has increased existing inequalities among sub-castes. For instance, the Chamars have been able to make better use of reservations and other policies for the weaker sections. The construction of Dalit identity has been their handiwork and they have been more active in both forms of assertion—grass roots activism and electoral politics. In contrast, the Balmikis, during the colonial and post-colonial period, underwent a process of Hinduization due to which they are less attracted towards Ambedkarization. The fault lines of Dalit unification are further exposed, as many lower castes like Dhobi, Pasi, Bhangi, etc., seldom use the word 'Dalit' to define themselves, since their individual caste identities are more significant for them. On the other hand, the smaller groups such as Jogi, Nat, Ranraj, Bhangi, Hela, Khatik, etc., remain miles away from the process of assertion. The BSP was initially viewed as a Chamar party and other sub-castes took some time to gravitate towards it. It was only from the mid-1990s that through political mobilization, the BSP has been able to overcome—but only in so far as voting is concerned—the social distance and increasing economic differentiation that identity formation and unequal development has created among Dalit groups (Pai 2002).

Tamil Nadu provides an example of intense division, competition, and even violent conflict among sub-castes at the grass roots. Caste dominance is fractured in the state with no single caste cluster that is socially, numerically or, politically pre-eminent—and each experiencing identity assertion and upward mobility—making it necessary to examine the separate histories of the different castes in understanding the volatile situation in the state. In fact, Pandian questions how far we can employ the terms BCs and Dalits—are Thevar and Vanniyar representatives of BCs in Tamil Nadu and similarly Devendars and Parayars of the Dalits? Among the latter, the Pallars (who have renamed themselves as the superior Devendar Kula Vellalars (DVK) feel they are superior to the Parayars who are not as advanced in the economic and educational field (Pandian 2001). They argue that when the Devendars are combined with other sub-castes, their struggles, history and, culture get concealed. A section of the DKV is constructing a new caste history in which Pallar is claimed to be a corruption of Mallar—chieftain of the irrigated tracts of the ancient Tamil region. The Delit Panther Iyakkam (DPI) has attempted to mobilize the Parayars first as Dalits, then the *cheri*-people, and now the downtrodden Tamils. Such identity-based demands are always combined with calls for more equitable distribution of resources. Each sub-caste increasingly calls itself by its caste name and takes pride in it. There is competition as well as attempts by each sub-caste group to show itself as higher than the other. For example, the Devendars claim that it was others who had placed them in degrading occupations such as drum beating, beef-eating, scavenging, etc. which led to violence between the Devendars and the Parayars in Puthupatti village in south Tamil Nadu in 1999 and 2000. In 1999, five Parayars belonging to the DPI were killed, and houses burnt and in 2000 the Parayars killed six Devendars of the PT (Pandian 2000).

Similarly, Thevars, Gounders, Naickers, and Vanniyars have pockets of dominance across the state and the Dalits have to confront them everywhere. Among these, Thevars and Vanniyars are two backward castes that have refused to submerge their specific identities in the non-Brahmin collectivities. The greatest conflict is between them and the Dalits. It is not the advanced sections but the less well to do among the BCs who are conflicting with the Dalits—caste identity seems to compensate for their marginalization in other areas. Thus, we cannot criticize all BC groups as oppressing the Dalits. Given the complexity, there is need to evolve a framework of analysis to address the marginalities of both the oppressor and the oppressed.

The emergence of sub-caste identity across many states has led to strident competition among sub-castes everywhere, best exemplified in the field of reservation. There have been demands for higher quotas for the more backward among the Dalits in a number of states. The BSP in 2001 proposed a 'most Dalit' quota of 6 per cent for the poorer and smaller sub-castes in Uttar Pradesh in proportion to their percentage in the population—this was also supported by other parties in the hope of gaining support (*The Times of India* 2001). In Bihar, Nitish Kumar has created a special category of 'Maha Dalit' in order to help the smaller and poorer sections, and has succeeding in gaining their support (Kumar 2012). The movement by the Madigas in Andhra Pradesh to provide a quota for all the sub-castes in the state, keeping with their economic status, has been violently opposed by the Malas who have been at the forefront of making use of reservations due to their better economic and educational position since the colonial period (Pai 2010). These divisions are most visible at the grass roots where different sub-castes remain separate from each other, which has weakened and divided the Dalit movement in all the states and the country.

★ ★ ★

The analysis indicates that assertion at the grass roots is the most significant form through which upper caste domination and oppression has been challenged by Dalits in recent years. This is because the working of the caste hierarchy is best observed at the village level where Dalits and the backwards confront each other. It is the landowning, middle, and backward caste groups—rather than the upper castes—that have emerged as the locally dominant castes and thereby the direct oppressors of Dalits at the village level. In a seminal study Mendelsohn observed that land and labour is no longer the source of power and prestige in rural India (Mendelsohn 1993). In fact, what we are witnessing is the gradual shift from a rural–agrarian occupational structure, in the case of Dalits, to one that is more diversified. Wherever this has occurred, it has freed Dalits from feudal control of the landlord over his livelihood, creating the potential to revolt against domination and oppression at the village level. While this process is still slow in Uttar Pradesh, it is occurring at a faster rate in Punjab and most particularly Tamil Nadu, which explains the differential nature of relationships and the levels of violence in these states.

Assertion at the grass roots has assumed different forms in different states. Uttar Pradesh presents an example of collective action, leading to increased political consciousness and identity building as part of Ambedkarization, an ideological trend with both cultural and economic aspects that has a long history in the western districts. In Punjab, in reaction to being treated as outcastes, Dalits have built their own religious and secular institutions of daily life, including livelihood, in an attempt to be equal to and yet separate from the upper and middle castes. In Tamil Nadu, educational and economic advancement among Dalits is much higher in some regions than that of backward caste groups, but the latter are not willing to accord equal social status and respect to the Dalits. This has resulted in intense anger and competition leading to high levels of violence and even to the return of older forms of untouchability.

At the same time, some common features are visible in this study of grass roots assertion in each of these states. First, it is part of the larger process of democratization through which Dalits become politically active and benefit—some Dalit sub-castes such as the Chamars in Uttar Pradesh and Punjab or Devendrars in Tamil Nadu who are more dominant have succeed in getting empowered faster—the process then moves downwards including the smaller and less politicized groups such as the Paraiyars in Tamil Nadu or the Kori or Dhobi in Uttar Pradesh who enter into the political mainstream. Second, while it has enabled Dalits to confidently challenge domination and oppression by the middle and backward castes, a dual process seems to be present: confrontation with the latter and at the same time a desire to become part of and be accepted by them as equal. It is hence a double-layered, multidirectional process, at times ambivalent and on other occasions highly confrontational. Third, assertion at the grass roots has led to tremendous violence as in Tamil Nadu. Conflict is not always a negative feature, it indicates that unequal power structures are being challenged and social change is taking place. This is evident from the fact that, unlike in the past, when Dalits suffered violence, today they are fighting back leading to caste riots which spreads over many days and across districts.

However, grass roots assertion despite its role in helping Dalits to deal with oppression, has created greater fragmentation and division among sub-castes leading to competition and at times confrontation. It was believed that the process of modernization which has accompanied democratization, and has touched the

Dalit community as well, would enable all citizens to overcome their narrow ethnic identities. However, the contrary has happened—sub-castes within the Dalit community have discovered and are asserting their narrow ethnic identities against not only the middle and backward castes, but against other Dalit sub-castes as well. This process is visible in many states: between the Malas and Madigas in Andhra Pradesh, Chamars and Balmikis in Uttar Pradesh, and the Devendrars and Parayars in Tamil Nadu. It has divided Dalits politically, with each group forming separate political parties, as in Tamil Nadu and had even led to violence. Thus, Dalit assertion at the grass roots is a complex phenomenon that has both helped take the Dalit movement forward, as well as created strong divisions within the Dalit community that have often been counterproductive.

3

Dalit Political Parties and Electoral Politics

Since the 1980s the emergence of Dalit-based parties, based on assertion from below, has been a significant political development. The Indian Constitution provided electoral reservations to the SCs to give a hitherto excluded social group—an opportunity to enter political institutions and to fashion leaders who would provide them leadership and a decisive share in political power. However, it is through mobilization in civil society, strong social movements, and establishment of political parties in recent years that Dalits have gained empowerment, entered politics, and even captured state power. Over the last two decades caste-based identities have driven state and electoral politics in the Hindi heartland—and in Maharashtra and Tamil Nadu—

where Dalits have formed parties of their own. Today there are many movements and organizations formed by Dalit leaders in civil society, some of which—as the previous chapter has shown—are active at the grass roots. However, there are only few established and recognized Dalit-based parties.

Traditionally, the Congress party had the electoral support of the Dalits in most states, particularly in north India. It was a party of the 'extremes', that is, the leadership was from the upper castes but the support base consisted of Dalits (Brass 1968). This was because the party was able to gain their support in the late colonial period—major exeptions being Tamil Nadu, Maharashtra, and Kerala—where strong social caste/ class-based movements led the Dalits to support parties such as the DMK and RPI, and the Left parties in Kerala. Since the 1980s, Dalit parties have become strong wherever the Congress has faced sharp decline, the best example being Uttar Pradesh. In states where the Congress has survived such as Madhya Pradesh, Andhra, Rajasthan, Punjab, and Haryana—despite considerable assertion at the grass roots—parties such as the BSP have entered, but despite concerted efforts have not been able to establish themselves. Thus in many parts of the country, the Congress has continued to gain the support of at least a section of the Dalits.

This chapter examines the working of four major Dalit-based parties: the RPI in Maharashtra and Uttar Pradesh, the BSP in Uttar Pradesh, and the DPI and the PT in Tamil Nadu. The aim is to understand both the specific characteristics of these parties and the impact they have had on electoral politics, the party system, and democracy.

Dalit Political Parties: Distinctive Features

Dalit-based parties are distinct from mainstream parties in terms of their roots, social base, value system, world view, strategies of mobilization, and goals. In Western Europe, parties arose as a response to the needs of representation within emerging parliaments, while in the developing world they arose mainly out of anti-colonial movements for independence. Dalit parties, in contrast, have their roots in anti-caste movements headed by Dalit leaders with a vision of creating an egalitarian society. These movements later converted into parties for electoral purposes, to capture power, owing to the centrality of the state in introducing change in India.

However, the conversion from movement to party remains incomplete making them 'movement-parties'. This often causes problems as movements aim at introducing social transformation by working at the grass roots, while parties are interested in capturing state power and introducing change, from above, using state power.

A key feature of Dalit parties is exclusivism, that is, they attempt to mobilize mainly Dalits and other weaker sections in order to gain political power and safeguard their socio-economic and political interests. As communitarian parties, they mobilize on identity lines and have a narrow social base, unlike mainstream parties most of which seek to mobilize a wider section of the electorate mainly on class lines. They do not have an ideology in the conventional sense, but are more concerned with providing equality, dignity, self-respect, and empowerment in the political sphere rather than material benefits. Dalit parties also practise the politics of symbolism by creating an alternative history through stories of past oppression and building statues and memorials of iconic Dalit leaders.

Due to these characteristics, Dalit-based parties are in essence both social movements as well as political parties. Beginning as movements, many of them decided over time to adopt the path of electoral competition due to dilemmas and compulsions that set them apart from mainstream parties (Pai 2002). First, Dalit emancipation is best served by joining mainstream parties such as the Congress—identified as the party which has provided Dalits protective discrimination and welfare—or forming an exclusively Dalit-based party. The former path has led many times to loss of autonomy and Dalits becoming a vote bank of the Congress party. The latter course is also problematic as such parties have a specific identity, and appeal to only a limited segment of the population, after which they tend to reach a plateau which they are are unable to move beyond and gain the votes of other sections of society. Second, if a separate party is to be formed, what kind of party will it be—an exclusively Dalit party that mobilizes along communitarian lines—or one which seeks support from all the weaker and disadvantaged sections of society? The former would make it a narrow sectarian party, limited to Dalits, while the latter would make it a party of the poorer sections leading to the loss of hard-won identity. Third, the agenda of Dalit upliftment can be fulfilled only if Dalit parties can capture state power. This drives them to look for alliances or coalitions with other parties, raising the question—should a Dalit-based party enter into alliances with only like-minded parties, or any party willing to support it in order to capture state power and gain control over public policy? While forming coalitions enables them to enter the corridors of state power—such cohabitation in power—with parties often representing conservative social forces, holds the danger of diluting their hard-won identity and even their social base. These dilemmas are visible in our analysis of the emergence and working of Dalit parties.

Liberal and Radical Dalit Parties in Maharashtra

The RPI was the first Dalit political party formed by the post-Ambedkar leadership in independent India. The death of Ambedkar in December 1956 delayed its formation to 22 April 1958. However, the Maharashtrian experience with Dalit political parties is unique in comparison with other states. Rather than forming a narrow communitarian party based on lower caste identity to obtain the support of Dalits, the state has experimented with two kinds of broad-based parties of the underprivileged: a Liberal Republican party that was meant to appeal to the entire working class and poor, and a Radical alternative, which sought to combine both caste and class through a Marxist-cum-Ambedkarite ideology. There was also a parallel emergence of *Dalit Sahitya* (literature of the oppressed) that highlighted the problems Dalits face in a hierarchical society. Although neither has succeeded electorally, there has been much social change in Maharashtrian society as a result of these experiments. The decline of these parties has affected the Dalit movement and also impacted on democratic politics in the state.

The RPI was formed by the working committee of the All India Scheduled Castes Federation (AISCF), which was formed by Ambedkar in 1942. The formation of the RPI took place at the site of the conversion to Buddhism in Nagpur and was attended by 3, 500 delegates from all over India (Gokhale 1990). A number of smaller organizations working against caste oppression since the 1940s also came together to form the party. Ambedkar had indicated the need for a broad-based liberal party of the weaker sections in his *Open Letter*. It was 'a limited version of the class model' and defined its support base very broadly: the Dalit classes, the Backward Classes, the peasant classes, the adivasis, the *nava buddha*s, the working classes, and landless labourers (Gokhale 1990: 247). Moreover, the party believed that the solution to the problems of the untouchables lay in social transformation of the society as a whole (Ibid.). Though formed as an All–India party with branches in some states, the RPI has had little presence in the Lok Sabha—three seats in 1962, one in 1967 and two in 1977 followed by no seats and less than 1 per cent of the vote. In 1998, there was a brief revival of the party when it won four seats (Table A.1). In the states, it had a presence only in Maharashtra and Uttar Pradesh, winning hardly one seat in each election in other states. It had a golden age during the late 1950s to early 1960s after which it experienced extreme divisions. Its best performance was in Uttar Pradesh as Table A.2 shows, during a period of Congress weakness, when it obtained a maximum of 10 seats and about 4 per cent of the votes in the 1967 elections. This dropped to just one seat in 1969 and 3.5 per cent of the votes (Baxter 1969). In Maharashtra it gained five seats in 1967 with 6.6 per cent of the votes and two seats in 1972 with 3.77 per cent of the votes, once again four seats in 1978 with a little over 2 per cent of the votes, after which it declined sharply both in terms of seats and votes. In 1985, it gained one seat and subsequently gained no seats. The party revived briefly in 1995 and 1999, winning one seat in each case, but with less than 1 per cent of the votes (Table A.2).

In keeping with its attempt to build a broad base, the RPI took up both class and caste-based issues (Gokhale 1990; Morkhandikar 1990). But its agitation did not attract the non-Dalit poor and it did not develop, as hoped, into a broader movement based on the support of the poorer sections. An important reason was that the leadership was not clear regarding the kind of party they had formed of the SCs only—or of all the poor leading to factionalism and constant splits. There were at least three to four factions of the party at any given time. The constitution of the party expected it to 'organize the peasantry, the landless labourers, workers in factories, and other wage earners'. Yet it also pledged to engage itself in organizing the downtrodden masses of India, particularly the Buddhists, SCs, STs, and OBC. In actual practice, it described itself as an Ambedkarite party and used a combination of caste and class mobilization in order to win votes (Duncan 1979: 236). Moreover, the Congress party using the politics of aggregation was able to attract a section of the RPI led by D.T. Rupwate and N.M. Kamble, while the rest of the party remained divided in factions that aligned with the opposition under R.S. Gawai and R. Khobragade (Morkhandikar 1990: 586).

The vacuum was filled by the rise of a more radical alternative in the early 1970s, the Dalit Panthers and the Dalit Sahitya (Gokhale-Turner 1979). The mid-1960s and early 1970s were a period of social discontent and economic travail—in Maharashtra and elsewhere—marked by inflation, the contraction of the job market, the women's movement and numerous strikes and demonstrations specially during the Emergency that hit young Mahar-Buddhists particularly hard. The experience had a radicalizing impact upon the small educated Dalit class in some states and led to formation of many militant groups—Karnataka Dalit Sangharsh Samiti, Andhra Dalit Mahasabha, a Dalit Panther unit in Gujarat, and the emergence of journals such as *Dalit Voice* by V.T. Rajshekar in Bangalore as well as Naxalite organizations in Bihar and elsewhere (Omvedt 1995). It is in this context that Raja Dhale and Namdev Dhasal formed the Dalit Panthers—as a radical, militant organization—drawing upon both Ambedkarite philosophy and Marxism. They drew their inspiration from the Black Panthers movement in the US and believed that violence could be used, if necessary (Kumar 2004). They described Congress rule as a continuation of Hindu feudalism (Omvedt 1995). Initially, they had no clear declared ideology and Ambedkar's vision served their needs until they brought out their own manifesto. The Dalit Panthers (DPs) in their 1972 manifesto defined Dalit as 'a member of SC and tribes, neo-Buddhist, the working people, the landless and poor peasants, women, and all those who are being exploited politically, economically, and in the name of religion' (Contursi 1993). The word Dalit among the DPs has a class connotation unlike in Uttar Pradesh where it is based purely on caste discrimination. Noted Maharashtrian Dalit writer Gangadhar Pantwane argues, 'Dalit is not a caste; Dalit is a symbol of change and revolution. The Dalit believes in humanism. He rejects existence of god, rebirth of soul, sacred books that teach discrimination, fate, and heaven, because these have made him a slave' (Ibid.).

However, the DPs faced problems early, as they could not resolve the central issue of Dalit identity. Was it to include all the oppressed sections of society or only the Dalits? Was it to include only the neo-Buddhists or all Hindu SCs? The Dhasal faction put forward a broad and inclusive class definition and became an ally of the Communists in Maharashtra— while the Dhale group—which took a narrower view of Dalit identity, considered itself as the only 'true Ambedkarites', that is, those who had converted to Buddhism and thereby shed their Dalithood and gained emancipation. Similarly, the Dalit Sahitya, being the product of the educated, urbanized, self-conscious middle class mahar Buddhist elite, had little to offer to the rural poor in the community (Murugkar 1991). Consequently, by the 1980s, the DPs came to be iden-tified as a group that indulged in much debate and discussion—but little action, alienating them from the uneducated poorer and rural Dalits in Maharasthra—thus making a return to electoral politics problematic (Morkhandikar 1990). This was also the assessment of Kanshi Ram when he visited them in Pune in the 1970s to look for a Dalit movement or party that he could join. The experience made Ram decide that, when he formed a party, it would be disciplined and spend less time on debate and more on organization and mobilization.

An attempt was made in 1984 to re-unite all factions of the RPI as the Bharatiya Republican Party of India (BRPI) under the leadership of Prakash Ambedkar, grandson of Dr Ambedkar (Morkhandikar 1990: 586–8). Based on a moderate liberal ideology and seeking an alliance with parties sympathetic to the Dalit cause, it took up many important issues in a bid to unite the Dalit community: a march from Nasik to Bombay demanding transfer of *vatan* lands to Dalit cultivators; formation of a *Vichar Samvardhak Samiti* against the government's decision not to publish Ambedkar's manuscript 'Riddles Of Hinduism' in his collected works, and the formation of a committee on 16 December 1989 to frame a constitution leading to launching of a new party during 5–6 January 1990. However, the unity moves proved unsuccessful and the RPI failed to get even a single seat in the 1989 parliamentary elections. In the Aurangabad municipal elections 1988, it gained three and the DPs two seats—but in the 1990 assembly elections Dalit votes were divided and only 1 out of 60 candidates put up by

Prakash Ambedkar won—while none of the 12 candidates of the other faction (led by Ramdas Athawale) was successful (Table A.2). In 1993, Prakash Ambedkar formed the Bahujan Mahasangh in 1993 as an extension of his BRPI in an attempt to bring together Dalits and OBCs under a Dalit initiative, but this was not successful.

Despite the failure of the RPI and the DPs to perform well in the electoral arena, it is undeniable that due to a long independent movement much change has taken place in Maharashtrian society. The Dalit Sahitya has provided the movement a literary underpinning and substitute for political involvement leading to considerable transformation and lower levels of conflict than in many other states (Gokhale 1990: 262). Although the DPs failed to introduce a radical edge to Dalit assertion in Maharahstra and the country, there have been attempts to bring together Marxism and Ambedkarism in the state. A good example is the story in the award-winning 200 minute documentary film *Jai Bhim Comrade* by well-known filmmaker Anand Patwardhan that took 14 years to complete and has been screened in 2012 in various *basti*s of Mumbai and many other towns. It films the the killing of Dalits and registration of false cases against them in 1997 in Ramabai Nagar. The movie shows the life of Vilas, a Dalit, and others like him who celebrated the life of Dr Ambedkar but also became Marxists leading to the consequent clash of identities (Borpujari 2013). The screening of the film has generated academic debate on the possibilities of political solidarities between the Dalit and the Left movements and the reasons for their failures (Natrajan, 2013).

But it cannot be denied that the Dalit movement in the state has run into serious problems. Dalits are divided along religious and class lines and along sub-castes lines of *Mang*s, *Mahar*s and *Chambhar*s with strong rivalries making a more inclusive identity such as Dalit difficult. An important factor is the absence of a leader like Ambedkar or Kanshi Ram. As a result, the Dalit voice in organized politics that provided strength has declined, and the number of caste attacks have increased, as witnessed in Akola in 2005 and Khairlanji in 2006. This has provided space to the Bhartiya Janata Party (BJP) and also the Shiva Sena that has grown in the state since the late 1980s, fracturing the RPI even further.

From Adi-Dravid to Dalit in Tamil Nadu

The 1980s was a decade of great social ferment in Tamil Nadu when Dalits rejecting Dravidian ideology and moved away to create autonomous politics and an independent identity (Pandian 1994a). Till then, despite occasional major differences, they had continued to support the Dravidian parties—the DMK and later the AIADMK (Geetha and Rajadurai 1993). During this decade, a number of Dalit organizations, some of them very radical in outlook and espousing both Marxism and Ambedkarism, emerged following violent clashes with the backward castes in parts of the state. The two main Dalit parties in Tamil Nadu today—the DPI and the PT—have their origins in these anti-caste organizations—they chose the path of 'institutional transformation' moving from being social movements to political parties (Gorringe 2005). While the mainstream discourse views Dalit parties as a mere extension of Dravidian politics, they actually arose in opposition to and as an alternative to Dravidianism and in response to the dilution of Periyarist ideals by the very parties that claimed to carry forward his legacy. A central idea that underlies the shift from movement to party is the notion of reclamation of rights in the public space compelling the Dravidian parties to accept the Dalits as political players. This has enabled the DPI and PT to claim space within urban and rural areas—at par with other parties as seen in wall posters, flagpoles, and murals—which has given them tremendous confidence (Ibid.).

As the Dalits are fragmented along sub-caste lines in the state, three main groups are involved in the formation of these parties and although they are represented throughout the state, their distribution is broadly mirrored by that of the earlier Dalit organizations. The DPI is strongest in the northern districts where Paraiyars are preponderant; PT in the south and west where Parayars are most numerous, while the Chakkiliars have yet to establish a movement. Each of these three Dalit groups is a caste category, which is divided into numerous sub-castes.

The DPI or the Liberation Panthers (Viduthalai Charithaigal) was formed in 1982 in Madurai by M. Malaichami and is currently led by R. Thirumavalavan, following the death of the former in 1990. Modelled on the DPs of Maharashtra, it was intended to be a radical alternative to many smaller groups that had emerged such as the Ambedkar People's Movement and the Radical Class movement. Its key motto is the Ambedkarite assertion: 'caste annihilation is people's liberation'. It was felt that the older movements had become 'political brokers or agents' and ignored the need for struggle against caste domination and untouchability. The DPI covers a large swathe of the state, stretching from Chennai—down to Virudhnagar and Cuddalore—across Perambalur and Dindigul. It has been active in the northern region supported by the Paraiyar youth. It appeals mainly to the Paraiyar sub-caste, but the determination to resist being branded a caste movement has led to significant numbers of Chakkiliyars and Pallars being drawn into the organization (Ibid.).

Under Thirumavalavan, the DPI changed its name to Liberation Panthers in 1999. Many argue that this was done to show sympathy with the Liberation Tigers of Eelam in Sri Lanka and to distinguish themselves from the DPs of Maharastra. In Tamil Nadu, it has also become increasingly a caste term associated with Parayar. More importantly, it is an attempt to avoid the term Dalit—which it is felt—was being over used and therefore has lost the radicalism associated with it and become an ascribed rather than a chosen epithet (Gorringe 2005). Despite this, the party flag and all its posters have an obligatory portrait of Ambedkar. The party has become well organized over the years with a convener and two general secretaries and cells, but most of branches are in the urban areas (Ibid.).

The DPI is issue-based in that it articulates a coherent set of principles and demands, but is also 'incident-based, that is, it reacts to the aggression of others rather than sustained campaigning on select issues (Ibid.) It is held that its success in attracting Dalits lies in its aggressive stance, and an articulate leadership with an attractive public image. It has militantly fought against untouchability, demanded equality in the public sphere, honour, self-respect, and dignity. The basic ideological stance of the DPI is a critique of the Dravidian parties for converting into simple regional parties for losing their anti-caste ideology and identity and converting into simple regional parties. This is considered to have brought the Brahmins back to a position of dominance in Tamil Nadu and ignoring of the problems faced by Dalits. Yet the party takes a stand on a range of issues that affect the lower castes: women's liberation,

Tamil history and nationalism, Buddhism, conversion, caste atrocities, globalization, oppression, exploitation of Muslims, and a better system of electoral reservations for Dalits.

The PT set up by Dr Krishnaswamy in 1995 also began as a social movement. A Coimbatore-based cardiologist, Krishnaswamy gave up his practice to fight for the Dalits and formed the Devendrar Kulla Vellalars Federation (DKVF)—an organization primarily made up of the Pallars to bring about social awakening and equality. The base of the organization is in areas where the Pallars are numerous such as the region from Tirunelveli to Coimbatore. In 1997, the Federation shifted from a movement to a full-fledged party. According to Krishnaswamy, the aim of the PT is social and economic emancipation of the Dalits by gaining a share in political power. Taking an Ambedkarite position, he argues that without political power Dalits cannot obtain social or economic power and must use every opportunity to seize power. The other main aim of the party is to remove untouchability and build bridges with other parties, particularly between Dalits and Thevars. Krishnaswamy is critical of the present electoral system, mainly with regard to reserved seats, which he feels does not provide adequate representation to Dalits and favours a system of proportional representation. His campaign for social justice has found support among the Muslims, Christians, fishermen, and other weaker communities. The PT has also supported trade unions, particularly the cause of casual workers and bonded labourers. The party argues that prior to initiating class struggle, the caste issue should be resolved—only after which the Dalits can join hands with other forces for the purpose of class struggle. It has led to greater consciousness among Dalits in the southern districts (Anandhi and Jayarajam 1999: 10).

Both the DPI and PT entered electoral politics in the 1990s. In 1996, Krishnaswamy was elected to the Tamil Nadu Assembly from the Ottapidaram (reserved) constituency in Tuticorin district as an independent candidate. Both parties together with some smaller parties and Muslim groups joined the TMC or Third Front formed prior to the June 1999 Lok Sabha elections. Thirumavalvaan claimed that the coming together of the BJP and the DMK posed a danger to TN. Thus this was the first time Dalit parties joined hands and decided to fight an election. This led to unprecedented violence in Chidambaram (reserved) constituency where Thirumavalavan stood against the PMK and the DMK. Dalits were prevented from voting in many places during the election. As Table A.2 shows, the DPI got no seats in the 1999 elections—about 2 per cent of the vote and Thirumavalavan lost. But he obtained 2,25,768 votes and stood second in a hard fought contest—the winning PMK candidate gained only a little over three lakh votes (Gorringe 2005). The impressive performance of Thirumavalavan signalled the autonomous consolidation of the Parayar votes in the northern districts.

In the 2001 Assembly elections both the parties decided to ally with the DMK. For the DPI, it was based on the Ambedkarite dictum of building alliances, to gain a share in political power, in order to destroy the capitalist and Brahminical system in the country. Thirumavalavan described the alliance as an attempt to enter the party in order to transform it from within while maintaining the autonomous political identity of the Dalits (Thirumavalavan 2003). In the 2001 elections, Thirumavalavan was elected to the Tamil Nadu Assembly while Dr Krishnaswamy lost his seat. One reason for both parties joining hands with the DMK is their antipathy to the AIADMK—which the DPI describes as the 'greater enemy' under the tyrannical and Brahminical leadership of Jayalalithaa. Both parties also have a strong antipathy towards the BJP as a Hindu party of the upper castes and were wary of joining hands with any alliance that had connections with the National Democratic Alliance (NDA) (Omvedt 2003: 15). In the 2004 Lok Sabha elections, the earlier alliances were not repeated, nor could the DPI or the PT join the Democratic Progressive Alliance formed by the DMK as Karunanidhi refused to allot seats to them. He promised to consider their case in the next Assembly elections, despite the fact that the two parties had supported the DMK in earlier elections and were keen on forming an alliance against the BJP. The DMK preferred to give seats to the PMK within the alliance—despite its desertion in 2001 in favour of the AIADMK—giving rise to much unhappiness among the Dalit parties. Isolated by the Dravidian parties, Thirumavalavan and Krishnaswamy formed an alliance of their own called the People's Front along with the Makkal Tamil Desam (MTD) and the Indian National League (INL), a Muslim party. The alliance contested

28 seats, and Thirumavalavan and Krishnaswamy fought elections from the Chidambaram and Tenkasi constituencies, but could not win any seats.

Thus the Dravidian parties attempt to marginalize the Dalit parties and form alliances with them only when they need their support. Initially the alliance with the DMK was a pragmatic move on the part of the Dalit parties to escape persecution and establish themselves as political players. However, they seemed to be increasingly buying themselves into the system and this transformed their leaders from 'figures of liberation to establishment figures' (Ibid.). The Dalit movement in Tamil Nadu has also failed to properly organize itself. Dalit parties still lack infrastructure, established secondary leaders, local offices, and sustained ideologically-driven campaigns. The Dalit movement is ideologically inspired but shaped by the imperatives of the present, responding to one crisis after another rather than building up an alternative. Thus, Dalit parties are caught up in everyday Tamil politics, with the result that the options open to them are limited to Tamil nationalism, idolization of Periyar at the rhetorical level, and the symbolic occupation of space. There will be a sense of autonomy only if the Dalit parties can stand apart from the Dravidian parties. (Karthikeyan 2009).

To maintain their hegemony, Dravidian parties use populist imagery, symbolism, and rhetoric—especially through the use of Tamil cinema and distribution of freebies such as TVs, laptops, mixer-grinders, and cheap or free rice while glossing over the ground realities of the disadvantaged sections. Elections have become vote-buying exercises in which much money is spent and where the culture of immediate rewards and populism reigns (Kartikeyan *et al.* 2012). The split of the DMK into two parties has further reduced space for third parties. Dalit parties need to get a fairly high share of the votes to win in each constituency—including reserved constituencies where non-Dalits tend to decide which Dalit will contest—and often win (Wyatt 2009).

A significant aspect that emerged in the late 1990s was a newly-emerging solidarity between the Dalits and the Muslims in the state. This is seen in the active participation by the Tamil Muslim Munnetra Kazhagam (TMMK)—a new party which is growing in popularity rivalling the older Muslim League—in an alliance against untouchability organized by the PT. This alliance is not on a firm footing yet and is opposed by the BJP and the Hindu Munnani as well as by the Thevars (Jeyranjan and Anandhi 1999: 15).

Dalit leaders today are attempting to introduce change and rethink their politics. The DPI has embarked on a process of wholesale restructuring in a bid to reach out to the mainstream. Unless this period of introspection results in a change of direction, Dalit politics will continue to be characterized by an emphasis on symbolism and identity. There are two problems. One is the divisions between sub-castes which prevent unity in the movement and second, the absorption of Brahminical values of hierarchy and untouchability by Dalits. Despite the rise of two parties through autonomous Dalit mobilization, the possibility of the two coming together, except occasionally during elections seems remote. The recent use of the Devendrar Kulla Vellalars (DKV) by the Pallars for self-definition, and its sanctification by the PT, marks out the Parayars and the Arunthiyars as caste inferiors. Krishnaswamy avoids the inclusive term Dalit and uses sub-caste or *jati* names in an obvious move to distinguish himself as the leader of the DKV.

A suggestion in recent years has been a Dalit–Left alliance with the Tamil Nadu Untouchability Eradication Front (TNUEF) organized by the Communist Party of India (Marxist) (CPI [M]). It is a direct product of the Dalit upsurge, but its approach is to deal with specific instances of untouchability rather than destroy the underlying structures of caste. In this context, a recent study discusses whether solidarities between the Dalit and Left movements are possible for an anti-caste politics—on what grounds does it become possible and whether both Left and Dalit movements are strengthened by such solidarity (Natrajan 2013). The study argues the need for an understanding of how 'difference' is produced and perpetuated by structures of power. It also requires an understanding of how this has to be brought about in creative ways as part of the struggle to annihilate the structures that produce and thrive upon difference' and transform them into inequality (Ibid.: 17). However, building such solidarities cannot come at the expense of denying the rights of Dalits and non-Dalits to occasionally work in different social spaces, and for the latter to be attentive to these needs. Further, the grounds for coming together cannot be wished into existence without seriously struggling with the difference that is historically structuring social relations across castes. Thus, clearly the process has been not easy in Tamil Nadu or elsewhere. In sum, Dalit parties in Tamil Nadu have established an 'institutional learning process' and are in an early phase of radicalism and enthusiasm and have yet to become established political forces. The larger Dalit movement is currently at the crossroads. Some sub-Dalit groups are just starting to mobilize and organize themselves, while existing Dalit parties are attempting to embrace the wider politics and identities of Tamil nationalism (Kartikeyan *et al.* 2012: 30).

From Harijan to Dalit Identity in UP

The RPI was the first Dalit party formed in Uttar Pradesh (UP) as early as 1956. A branch of the all-India RPI formed after the death of Ambedkar, it proved to be a marginal party in the state for a brief period (Pai 2002). As Table A.2 shows, it obtained a maximum of ten seats and about 4 per cent of the votes in the 1962 and 1967 elections, which dropped to only two seats in 1969 and 3.5 per cent of the votes. Its success was due to weakness of the Congress in the

mid–1960s and an electoral alliance with Muslim organizations in four districts of western UP. The RPI's
seats were limited to a few districts, and before it could
spread to others, it disappeared. A major reason was
the lack of political consciousness—the large mass of
SCs remained trapped within the larger Hindu identity, unaware of their distinct Dalit identity. Unlike
in Maharashtra, it disappeared in the 1970s and was
absorbed by the Congress—which as the party with a
base among the Dalits—left little space for a separate
Dalit party until its decline and defeat in 1989.

The BSP was formed in 1984 more than 30 years
after independence—and unlike the RPI—has a definite self-identity, strong and assertive leadership, and
distinct social base. It is a product of post-Independence
developments: a long-term process of democratization,
policies of affirmative action, and rise in literacy among
Dalits particularly between 1981–91 which helped in
the sharp increase of political consciousness and the
decline of the Congress system which provided space
for narrower identity-based parties. Equally important
was the improvement in the agrarian economy in parts
of Uttar Pradesh that contributed to change in rural
social relations and the emergence of low-caste identity.

This provided the potential to revolt, particularly against the landowning middle and backward castes (Pai 2002). The roots of the BSP—its ideology, leadership, and organization—are different from other militant Dalit movement or parties such as the DPs in Maharashtra and the Dalit Sangharsh Samiti in Karnataka. It arose out of a middle class trade union organization of government employees—the BAMCEF—formed in 1976 by Kanshi Ram made up of the educated and better-off groups among the Dalits. As a result, the BSP is not a movement emerging from civil society against the state; rather it is a 'Statist' party. It believes in providing social justice and tries to uplift the Dalits from above using the power of the state rather than a revolution from below. Even during an early period, when it was a militant movement, it stayed out of many major Dalit struggles such as the Namantar agitation for renaming the Marathawada University (Guru 1994; Punalekar), the desecration of Ambedkar's statue in Bombay in July 1998, and in Shergadi in Meerut in 1993 (Pai 2002). In this sense, the BSP is different from the RPI which was much more an Ambedkarite party with an ideological bent—it was also a movement that tried to work for the upliftment of Dalit and non-Dalit poor, and the creation of identity consciousness, rather than only concentrating on gaining political power.

The BSP began as a social movement but entered the political arena as a political party in the late 1980s and has steadily increased its seat and vote share in Uttar Pradesh, as seen in Table A.2. Its success has been due to its ability to constantly adjust its mobilizational strategies and developmental agenda to the rapidly changing political scene in Uttar Pradesh, and at the same time, retain and consolidate its core support base among the Dalits. It has been through a number of phases: an early phase of militant mobilization between 1985 and 1993 when the BSP emphasized on its distinct character as a Dalit-based party or movement, kept a distance from other parties, characterized both Gandhi and mainstream parties as *Manuvadi*, and opposed Hindutva and caste-based atrocities. During the second phase, it attempted an alliance with the Samajwadi Party (SP), another lower caste party, to form a 'Bahujan Samaj'. As Table A.2 shows, together the two were able to defeat the BJP and win the 1993 assembly elections. However, the coalition failed by 1995, revealing problems of long-term import, which has prevented the two from joining hands again. In rural areas, the SP has the support of the landowning middle castes and the Jats, while the base of the BSP has a substantial number of landless Dalits. Today, they also compete for reservations in government employment and education. Consequently, rather than the Brahmins, it is the middle castes who constitute the direct oppressors of the Dalits (Pai 2002). The BSP was conceived as a Bahujan party which would unite the backwards and Dalits against the upper castes, but after 1995 it became specifically a Dalit party. Described in the early 1990s by the *Balmikis* and *Pasi* as a 'Chamar' party; by the end of the decade, the BSP was able to consolidate votes of all the sub-castes (Ibid.).

The failure of the SP–BSP coalition inaugurated a 'post-bahujan phase' in which the BSP adopted strategies to widen its social base and gain state power. These strategies included coalitions and electoral alliances with upper caste parties and giving tickets to non-Dalits from the backward classes. The party leadership described the coalition with the BJP in 1995 and in 1997 as a temporary and tactical method to gain power—a form of mobilization—encouraging Dalits to stand up for their rights and support the BSP. Mayawati, as Chief Minister used her period in office to implement a number of socio-economic and cultural policies exclusively for the Dalits—and to a lesser extent—for the backward classes and the Muslims. However, both coalitions proved short-lived due to constant friction over the policies followed by Mayawati. The electoral alliance with the Congress prior to the 1996 elections did not provide any significant gains as a hung Assembly emerged (Table A.2). Instead, the policy of giving tickets to non-Dalits in order to widen its social base and to ensure 'quicker growth' and 'empowerment of the oppressed' proved more successful particularly in the 1999 parliamentary elections in which the BSP gained 14 seats (Table A.1). Thus by the end of the decade, the BSP could consolidate the vote of the Dalits and sections of the backward, and emerge as a strong party. In contrast, the BJP which formed coalitions with the BSP during the 1990s underwent a sharp decline and the Congress was unable to revive itself. This created a bipolar system in the first decade of the twenty-first century in which two lower caste parties—the BSP and the SP—are competing for power in UP.

Since the 1990s, the BSP has also used the politics of symbolism to strengthen its Dalit base. This has been through building the building of statues, memorials and parks named after Ambedkar, the latest being the park in Noida which has statues of important Dalit icons starting from Jyotiba Phule. It has also renamed districts in UP after Buddha, Shahu Maharaj, and new histories of Dalit heroes have been written to give the Dalits a sense of pride (Narayan 2006). Local women heroes have also been identified—such as Jhalkaribai, Udadevi, and Avantibai who are believed to have played a historic role in the past—some in the 1857 mutiny (Ibid.). While Mayawati's recent building of statues in Noida has been criticized by the middle class and political leaders—and even some sections of Dalits, as a waste of funds which could have been used for development—the Dalit masses seem to have appreciated it.

With the weakening of primordial identities in Uttar Pradesh, the BSP has attempted to redefine itself from an avowedly Dalit to a *sarvajan* party (Pai 2007). A major shift took place in the strategies of the BSP prior to the 2007 Assembly elections. Instead of giving a large number of tickets to non-Dalits, it attempted to gain the support of the twice-born castes by approaching and mobilizing them directly. With the continued decline of the BJP and the Congress, the upper castes—

particularly the Brahmins—were in search of a party which they could join (Kumar 1999). The BSP held a number of Brahmin *sammelans* during the campaign for the 2007 elections in which Mayawati promised to not only give more tickets to Brahmins but also Cabinet positions. The main aim of the BSP was to build a system similar to the erstwhile combine of the upper castes, Dalits, and Muslims that had enabled the Congress party to rule UP over a long period. This would allow the party to overcome its inability to capture power alone and yet build a social combine in which the Dalits were in a commanding position.

In the 2007 Assembly elections the BSP gained an absolute majority, for the first time, obtaining 206 seats and 30.45 per cent of the votes. This is shown in Table A.2. However, the SP managed to retain its social base, getting 25.43 per cent of the votes (almost the same as in 2002), but it obtained about 46 seats less because the BSP was able to consolidate the anti–SP vote. The SP gained almost 8 per cent at the expense of the BJP that lost over 3 per cent, and to a lesser extent the Congress that experienced a decline of half a per cent (Table A.2). Though the BSP was able to capture power, it now faced the formidable challenge of balancing the expectations of the upper castes and other social groups that helped vote it to power, as well as the demands of its core constituency, the Dalits. The upper castes would not hesitate to return to the Congress or BJP if their expectations of a share in both political power and economic growth were not fulfilled. At the same time Dalits would no longer be satisfied with self–respect, dignity, and empowerment and would expect that the BSP leadership would make efforts to fulfil their long standing needs and aspirations. There was also the larger issue of whether the BSP—having tried to broaden its base to include the upper castes—could at the same time retain its identity as a Dalit party or movement (Pai 2009).

On assuming office, Mayawati made it clear that based on the agenda of sarvajan, the focus of her government would be the welfare of all sections, and not just Dalits. This was reflected in the caste composition of her ministry which included a number of Brahmins and the adoption of an agenda of rapid economic development for all social groups and backward regions of the state. Mayawati identified the 'priority areas' of her government as 'rural development, agriculture, social development, and infrastructure, making the state conducive for attracting investment' and sought massive economic assistance from the Centre. The BSP government in contrast to the retributive social justice agenda of the past, spent considerable amount of its budget on health, education, housing, social security, health, and education (Singh 2010). However, there were some trends from the past that continued due to uncomfortable signals from Dalits, after Mayawati's increasing emphasis on Brahmins during the elections and in her first two months in power. This is evident from the politics of symbolism—manifested in vast funds spent on statues and memorials in the state honouring Dalit icons—and the adoption of policies specifically for Dalits. A good example was the 'Mukhya Mantri Mahamaya Garib Arthik Madad Yojna' launched on 1 November 2010 for the poorest of the poor to meet their daily needs.

Elections since 2007 have thrown up contrary results. The BSP won all the three Assembly and two Lok Sabha seats in the by-elections held in April 2008. The Congress, SP, and BJP were badly defeated—but more importantly—victories in key constituencies clearly demonstrated that the Muslims and Brahmins still supported the BSP. In contrast, in the 2009 Lok

Sabha elections—as Table A.1 shows—the BSP failed to improve over its earlier position of 19 seats, there were signs of revival of the Congress party, and the SP slipped from its high of 35 seats, though it continued to remain the party with the highest number of seats. Yet signals from the grass roots seemed to suggest that the BSP had retained its hold over its Dalit constituency. The party virtually swept the panchayat polls held in late October 2010 with BSP-supported independent candidates winning the maximum seats (Verma 2012). Despite this, in the 2012 Assembly elections as Table A.2 shows, the BSP could gain only 80 seats and 25.9 per cent of the votes, which was a drop of about 5 per cent from 2007. The results suggest that despite efforts, the BSP did not seem to have successfully balanced the political and economic expectations of both the upper castes and the Dalits leading to its less than expected performance.

The BSP undoubtedly has a number of seminal achievements to its credit. It has carried forward the democratic revolution for the Dalits. It has created a new identity in place of the Varna system and a counter-ideology to 'Ambedkarism'. This has succeeded in removing the hold of Brahminical ideology and boosted the morale of the Dalits, providing them with a new confidence and self-respect (Pai 2002: 10). These achievements have broken down the vertical patron–client relationship with the upper castes, the accompanying political mobilizational pattern of vote banks, and constructed new solidarities on a horizontal dimension. But it has not been able to realize its full potential. It has not been a democratizing or empowering experience for the vast mass of subaltern Dalits in the state (Ibid.). Since the early part of first decade of the twenty-first century, it has attempted to transform itself into a broad-based umbrella party with a Dalit core. It remains to be seen, if this can take the Dalit movement in Uttar Pradesh and the country forward.

★ ★ ★

Dalit parties are the outcome of social movements in civil society by Dalit leaders. In all states there has been institutionalization of Dalit movements into political parties over the last two decades. The reasons for this shift have been critically debated by scholars. Dalit leaders have argued that social transformation through movements would take a long time—whereas capture of state power would lead to faster empowerment of

Dalits—enable them to resist oppression and introduce policies favourable to Dalits from above. In this attempt, Dalit parties have also given tickets to non-Dalits, formed alliances with mainstream parties, and sought support of the upper castes to widen their electoral base as Dalits form a small percentage of the population in the states. These strategies draw on the Ambedkarite dictum that political power is the key to social change.

The rise of Dalit parties has had a positive impact on electoral politics, the party system, and democracy in the country. While earlier electoral politics was the preserve of upper castes and mainstream parties, the rise of Dalit parties has introduced greater social inclusiveness into the political system. The collapse of the single-party Congress system—which despite an upper caste leadership—had a strong vote bank among the Dalits—has provided space for the rise of many smaller parties based on identity. Earlier many Dalits were not allowed to exercise their franchise. However, with the emergence of Dalit parties, the spread of the power of the vote has been an empowering process bringing them into the political mainstream. At the same time, Dalit parties have continued to mobilize the poorer and smaller Dalit sub-castes and the process of democratization has accompanied the electoral process in percolating downwards to include these marginal groups. A good example is the BSP which has been able to widen and consolidate its Dalit base, earlier limited to the Chamars, despite differences among sub-castes in UP.

However apart from UP, where a single party has been able to unite large sections of the Dalits, the hope that politics would be a unifying force has been belied. In Maharashtra and Tamil Nadu, Dalit-based parties have not been able to bring Dalits onto a single political platform. In Maharashtra, despite many attempts at revival, the RPI remains divided—between the neo-Buddhists and Hindu Dalit on one hand—and the Mahars and other sub-castes on the other, accompanied by intense factionalism among the leadership. In Tamil Nadu, Dalit parties have been formed along sub-caste lines, which have created deeper divisions, antagonism, and even violence. The question of what a political party means to Dalits has also been raised. Many have expressed disillusionment as Dalit parties have promised self-respect and dignity, but have not been able to provide economic betterment despite achieving political power, as in UP.

This brings us to the larger issue of whether the formation of Dalit parties has helped in creating greater unity within the Dalit movement or if it has taken forward the fight for equality and social transformation.

Dalit parties have emphasized more on political empowerment, with less stress on social status, removal of discrimination, and economic improvement. Neither Dalit movements nor parties have been anti-systemic forces—nor have they tried to challenge and transform the basic structure of the Indian social system— replacing caste and the accompanying social oppression, economic exploitation, and political domination by an egalitarian society. Rather, Dalit parties have made compromises with mainstream parties in their attempt to come to power through pre-electoral alliances as in Tamil Nadu and Maharashtra, or post-electoral coalitions in UP. It has been argued, that these strategies have helped in empowering Dalits and providing them greater confidence and a position within mainstream politics. In reality, it has helped only the already better-off groups. The benefits have yet to reach subaltern Dalit groups that remain poor, marginalized, and without a voice in the democratic system.

Appendix

TABLE A.1 Performance of Dalit Parties in the Lok Sabha Election (1962–2009)

Party	1962	1967	1971	1977	1980	1984	1989	1991-92	1996	1998	1999	2004	2009
REP/RPI	3★ 2.83%	1★★ 2.47%	1★★★ 0.49%	2# 0.59%	0 0.37%	0 0.08%	0 0.20%	0 0.04%	0 0.01%	4^ 0.37%	0 0.18%	1^^ 0.18%	0
BSP						–	3> 2.07%	3	11>> 4.02%	5@ 4.67%	14@@ 4.16%	19@@@ 5.33%	21★& 6.17%
DPI											0	0	–
PT										0 0.16%	0	In alliance	0 0.40%

Source: Election Commission of India (www. eci. nic. in).

Notes: ★ All (1 reserved seat for SC; 2 general seats) in UP.

★★ SC reserved seat in UP.

★★★ In Maharashtra

1 (reserved seat) in Maharashtra and 1 (general seat) in MP.

> 2 (1 reserved seat; 1 general seat) in UP and 1 in Punjab.

>> 6 (4 unreserved seats; 2 reserved seats) in UP.

^ In Maharashtra.

^^ In Maharashtra.

@ 4 (2 unreserved seats; 2 reserved seats) in UP.

@@ All (5 reserved seats for SC; 9 general seats) in UP.

@@@ All (5 reserved seats for SC; 14 general seats) in UP.

*& 20 (2 reserved seats for SC/ST; 18 general seats) in UP and 1 in MP.

TABLE A.2 Performance of Dalit Parties in Assembly Elections in Three States

State	Year	Political Parties	Number of seats contested	Number of seats won (Vote %)
Uttar Pradesh	1962	Republican	123	8 (3.74)
	1967	Republican Party of India (RPI)	168	10 (4.14)
	1969	Republican Party of India (RPI)	172	1 (3.48)
	1974	Republican Party of India (Ambedkarite)(RPA)	1	0 (0.00)
		Republican Party of India (RPI)	52	0 (0.31)
		Republican Party of India (Khobragade) (RPK)	87	0 (0.50)
	1977	Republican Party of India (RPI)	11	0 (0.08)
		Republican Party of India (Khobragade) (RPK)	40	0 (0.28)
	1980	Republican Party of India (RPI)	2	0 (0.01)
		Republican Party of India (Kamble) RPI(K)	1	0 (0.02)
		Republican Party of India (Khobragade) (RPK)	26	0 (0.16)
	1985	Republican Party of India (RPI)	1	0 (0.00)
	1989	Bahujan Samaj Party (BSP)	372	13 (9.41)
		Republican Party of India (RPI)	21	0 (0.00)
	1991	Bahujan Samaj Party (BSP)	386	12 (9.44)
		Republican Party of India (RPI)	16	0 (0.02)

1993	Bahujan Samaj Party (BSP)	164	67 (11.12)
	Republican Party of India (RPI)	25	0 (0.06)
	Republican Party of India (Democratic) RPI(D)	9	0 (0.02)
	Republican Party of India (Kamble) RPI(K)	1	0 (0.00)
1996	Bahujan Samaj Party (BSP)	296	67 (19.64)
	Republican Party of India (RPI)	23	0 (0.03)
2002	Bahujan Samaj Party (BSP)	491	91 (23.06)
	Republican Party of India (RPI)	25	0 (0.03)
2007	Bahujan Samaj Party (BSP)	403	206 (30.03)
	Republican Party of India (RPI)	12	0 (0.01)
	Republican Party of India (A) RPI(A)	14	0 (0.01)
2012	Bahujan Samaj Party (BSP)	403	80 (25.91)
	Republican Party of India (A) RPI(A)	53	0 (0.06)
	Republican Party of India (RPI)	10	0 (0.01)
	Republican Party of India (Democratic) RPI(D)	02	0 (0.00)
Maharashtra	Republican	66	3 (5.38)
1962	Republican Party of India (RPI)	79	5 (6.66)
1967	Republican Party of India (RPI)	118	2 (3.77)
1972	Republican Party of India (RPI)	25	2 (1.06)
1978	Republican Party of India (Khobragade) (RPK)	23	2 (1.41)

Table A.2 (*contd*)

State	Year	Political Parties	Number of seats contested	Number of seats won (Vote %)
	1980	Republican Party of India (RPI)	36	0 (0.76)
		Republican Party of India (Khobragade) (RPK)	42	1 (1.36)
	1985	Republican Party of India (RPI)	54	0 (1.00)
		Republican Party of India (Khobragade) (RPK)	16	0 (0.52)
	1990	Bahujan Samaj Party (BSP)	122	0 (0.42)
		Republican Party of India (RPI)	21	0 (0.70)
		Republican Party of India (Balakrishnan) RPI(B)	1	0 (0.00)
		Republican Party of India (Khobragade) (RPK)	18	1 (0.50)
	1995	Republican Party of India (RPI)	61	0 (0.15)
		Republican Party of India (Khobragade) RPI(K)	13	0 (0.17)
		Bahujan Samaj Party (BSP)	145	0 (1.49)
	1999	Republican Party of India (RPI)	10	1 (0.69)
		Republican Party of India (Khobragade) RPI(KH)	1	0 (0.00)
		Bahujan Samaj Party (BSP)	83	0 (0.39)

2004	Republican Party of India (RPI)	4	0	(0.15)
	Republican Party of India (A) RPI(A)	20	1	(0.49)
	Republican Party of India (Democratic) RPI(D)	18	0	(0.03)
	Republican Party of India (Kamble) RPI(KM)	2	0	(0.00)
	Bahujan Samaj Party (BSP)	272	0	(4.00)
2009	Republican Party of India (RPI)	6	0	(0.10)
	Republican Party of India (A) RPI(A)	79	0	(0.85)
	Republican Party of India (Democratic) RPI(D)	15	0	(0.02)
	Republican Party of India (Kamble) RPI(KM)	5	0	(0.00)
	Republican Party of India Ektawadi (RPIE)	1	0	(0.02)
	Bahujan Samaj Party (BSP)	281	0	(2.35)
Tamil Nadu	1962	Republican (REP)	4	0	(0.45)
	1967	Republican Party of India (RPI)	13	0	(0.20)
	1977	Republican Party of India (RPI)	4	0	(0.02)
	1980	Republican Party of India (RPI)	4	0	(0.04)
	1991	Republican Party of India (RPI)	3	0	(0.00)
	1996	Republican Party of India (RPI)	5	0	(0.05)
	2001	Puthita Tamilagam (PT)	10	0	(1.27)
		Republican Party of India (RPI)	3	0	(0.00)
	2011	Puthita Tamilagam (PT)	2	2	(0.40)

Source: Based on election results in three states drawn from relevant reports of the Election Commission of India.

4

Dalit Middle Class Activism

In recent years, the Dalit movement has taken a different turn. As earlier chapters have shown, a strong
wave of assertion was harnessed during the 1980s
by a vanguard of educated middle class Dalit leaders
who were able to provide leadership to the poorer but
politically conscious and upwardly mobile sections
of the community, and enter the political field. Since
the late 1990s, we have witnessed the emergence
of new forms of political activism by a small, better
educated, influential, and younger generation Dalit
middle class. This new class which forms a small elite
section within the Dalit community is also a product
of the processes of democratization, Dalit assertion, and
state policies of protective discrimination discussed
earlier. An additional significant factor is globalization,

rise of the private sector, and higher growth of the Indian economy. However, arguably the impact of this new class on Dalits and Indian democracy has been different.

This chapter attempts to identify some of the specific characteristics of the new Dalit middle class, which distinguishes them from a previous generation that was active in mass and electoral politics during the 1980s and 1990s. It also focuses upon a key issue that this new class has been stridently engaging with: re-examining the traditional policy of reservation provided in the Constitution—its achievements, limits, and continued usefulness in the new context of globalization. The new middle class espouses new notions regarding social justice and strongly feels that the role of the state, market, and civil society in helping Dalits enter the social, economic, and political mainstream needs to be redefined. These ideas shape their political activism through which they advocate two forms of affirmative action for Dalits: extension of the traditional policy of reservations to the private sector and a share in business and industry through policies based on the principles of 'democratization of capital' and diversity. The concluding section comments on the usefulness of these new ideas and policies and what it means for Dalits in India.

Emergence and Ideological Moorings

In recent years, many studies have focused on the rise of an Indian middle class in the context of globalization (Fernandes 2007). However, little attention has been paid to the new Dalit middle class, whose roots, needs, and aspirations are arguably different. Gyanendra Pandey has recently questioned whether there can be a 'subaltern middle class' among the Dalits in India and the 'black bourgeoisie' in the USA as they belong to a long-stigmatized lower caste and underclass in these two locations (Pandey 2009). In fact, the notion of 'middle classness' itself underwent considerable mutation in its passage from the European to the developing world. He points out that it is not wealth or inheritance but education, self-improvement, effort, and sheer determination that bring advancement to the individual, family, and society. The members of the new Dalit middle class being discussed, are aware of the long history of struggle and the limits and necessary conditions for the emergence and consolidation of Dalits as part of the modern and de-stigmatized middle class. Hence, they desire to formulate new policies or programmes of affirmative action for advancement of Dalits— supported by the state, civil society, and market in the new context of a globalizing economy.

This chapter argues that this new generation Dalit middle class represents a different strand in the Dalit movement as it evolved in the last few decades (Pai 2010a). While Dalit movements and parties, discussed in earlier chapters, were mobilized by political leaders on issues of political empowerment such as identity, dignity, and self-respect—the new middle class Dalit intellectuals emphasize on the need for economic empowerment through a variety of new methods. A major characteristic of this class is better educational levels—an increasing number of English educated individuals occupy senior ranks within the bureau-cracy including public sector undertakings though fewer numbers are found in academia and business. As Sheth has argued, there has been 'classization of caste', that is, a largely urban and economically better-off section has emerged among Dalits and which is different from its rural brethren. Even in rural areas, a recent questionnaire-based survey administered to all Dalit households in two blocks in Azamgarh and Bulandshahar districts in eastern Uttar Pradesh, focused specifically on changes since 1990 in a variety of caste practices at the household and social level. The survey found marked changes in living styles, migration patterns, educational levels, social relationships with upper castes in the village, and most importantly—change in employment patterns with Dalits shifting to urban areas and moving to new and better-off sectors of the economy (Kapur *et al.* 2010). Though such changes are not widespread in Uttar Pradesh or elsewhere, but these are still indications of changes taking place and the new aspirations and ambitions among younger Dalits.

However, what is significant for our study is that this class reached a 'critical mass' precisely when the Indian polity experienced globalization moving towards a market-oriented economy. Consequently, this new class shares the anger of their more disadvantaged brethren against the continued oppression and domination by the upper castes and classes. But this class also strongly feels that it should receive a fair share in the fruits of post-Independence political and economic development—particularly following globalization—which has resulted in higher growth rates, a market economy, and emergence of a strong private sector with highly-paid professional and business opportunities. Hence, it is interested in discussing and formulating new policies of affirmative action and pressuring the state, civil society, and corporate sector for acceptance, and has distanced itself from political mobilization. Consequently, it must be distinguished from the identity-based movements and parties whose aim is capture of state power; or the Dalit Panthers of Maharashtra who in the early 1970s represented a radical intellectual group based on the ideological combination of Marxism and Ambedkarism.

The emergence of this class has initiated a contentious debate among Dalit and non-Dalit scholars/ activists on the working of reservation policies in the post-Independence period, the benefits that have accrued to them, and the new types of preferential policies that are required so that Dalits can reap the benefits of globalization. They point out that under the traditional policies of protective discrimination and state welfare, the large majority of Dalits have remained mere recipients of welfare, without land or assets, below the line of poverty, without a share of capital in the economy, and unable to improve their socio-economic status. While a tiny elite 'creamy layer' has emerged which has been able to gain high paid jobs in the government and increasingly the private sector—the poorer sections have been unable to access education and therefore cannot avail reservation policies. The educated section who have been able to obtain 12 years of schooling or college degrees have, on an average, been able to enter low paid jobs, mainly in the government. They have not been able to enter areas which are becoming important in India's globalized economy such as the IT and services sector, and have remained on the fringes of the expanding professional market. Nor have many educated Dalits been able to enter into sectors such as the media, arts, academia, scientific establishment, or business and industry.

The ideas of the new Dalit middle class are best understood by looking at the Bhopal Document (BD) and the Dalit Agenda within it, which emerged from a gathering of Dalit intellectuals and activists in Bhopal in January 2002 (Babu 2003; Nigam 2002). The BD had its roots in the late 1990s in the attempt by a group of Dalit intellectuals and activists to present to the Congress party—a report focusing on the socio-economic conditions of Dalits and a set of proposals that would go beyond the conventional state policies for this social category. The report had its immediate origins in the 'Dalit Millennium'—one of the 'Millennium Supplements' issued by *The Pioneer*—to mark the dawn of the millennium on 30 January 2000. A well-conceived supplement consisting of about 12 pages, it was edited by a young Dalit Indian Administrative Services (IAS) officer R.S. Vundru who put together the views of several Dalit intellectuals, academics, journalists, and fellow IAS officers. It dealt with a wide range of issues of significance for Dalits: problems in reservation, the controversial issue of merit, representation in state institutions such as the judiciary, need for better educational attainments, leadership, caste atrocities, plight of Dalit women, etc. Some articles discussed the need for 'diversification of Dalits from government service to other fields', others 'correction of land-labour relations', and a few focused on the need for a new 'Dalit Bourgeoisie' in the field of business and industry. The 12-page broadsheet received critical acclaim and was instrumental in bringing together the individuals who produced it and the leaders of the Congress government of Madhya Pradesh—making the Bhopal Conference possible on 30 January 2002. The conference was a historic attempt to bring together for the first time, the middle class, educated Dalit (and tribal) intellectuals and activists and representatives of the state to discuss the emerging situation due to democratization and globalization, the resultant problems faced by these groups, and policies to meet them (Pai 2010b).

The Bhopal Conference discussed at length the need for a new societal consensus emerging from dialogue between the dominant and disadvantaged groups on the Dalit question. The conference members raised a number of larger issues: Can Indian society become a genuine democracy without democratizing its traditional social, cultural, and political institutions; can it evolve into a civil society without eliminating its Varna or caste hierarchies? (The Bhopal Document 2002: 30). Pointing to 'a possible tension between universalistic aspiration of social democracy and the particularity of the discourse of caste' the BD argues that the reality of caste had impeded the creation of a genuinely universalistic aspiration of social democracy in at least two ways. First, too great an insistence on the caste question

124

creates divisions amongst groups that might otherwise be possible allies for the democratization of civil society. Second, the discourse on caste seems to allow for the slow co-option of even sub-groups amongst the Dalits. The report identifies the 'upper varnas' and 'upper shudras' as the two dominant blocks that own most of the nation's assets and public institutions. It avoids criticizing Brahminism directly and depicts a broader picture of the sources of Dalit oppression (Bhopal Document 2002: 30). Further the BD holds that change will have to be 'more evolutionary than revolutionary', non-conflicting, taking into consideration the existing opinions in society—both Dalit and non-Dalit (Ibid.: 59.) Critical of leaders of movements or parties such as the BSP who hold that unless Dalits capture state power nothing can be achieved, it pointed out that these movement and parties have provided 'political rights' but have had little impact on the economic condition of Dalits (Ibid.: 37). Thus the declaration, while it supported the cause of Dalits—tried to position them as bearers of a more universal agenda, rising above the narrow caste politics engulfing the country. It realized that to obtain freedom from caste, it will have to break open the confines of caste politics as well. Thus, the BD represents a middle-class-driven attempt at change.

Based on these ideas, the conference examined the continued usefulness of older policies such as protective discrimination and proposed new policies and programmes for Dalits in the changed context. The BD portrays disillusionment with the Indian state which restricted its role to implementing policies for Dalits such as reservations, poverty alleviation programmes, scholarships to students, and loans, etc., which did not improve their socio-economic status. It is critical of the 'excessive belief' in reservations which has 'shaped the consciousness of the SC/ST masses' and various forms of state welfare as the 'overriding phenomenon' and the 'most decisive tool of progress' for Dalits. It raised the seminal question: where will Dalits be by AD 2100? Pointing out that it is necessary to realize that there are limits to reservations, the document cogently argues that even if the existing job quota available in the government under reservations were to be filled, a large number of SCs/STs would still be without employment. According to the Annual Report of the Union Ministry of Labour, 2000–1, the total number of jobs under the state (Union Government, public sector undertakings [PSUs], state governments, local bodies) is 1.94 crore. This means that if the total existing quota of 22.50 per cent reservations is given to SCs/STs, the total number of Dalit employees cannot go beyond 45 lakh. If we multiply this figure by five (assuming that every SC/ST employed under the state caters to a family of five), it shows that the benefits cannot reach beyond a population of 2.25 crore. This still leaves as many as 18 crore Dalits still seeking employment. Thus while education is seen as the path of emancipation, government employment through reservations is not possible for all. The total employment available in the private sector according to the annual report is about 86.98 lakh. If the private sector were to religiously implement reservations, it would lead to an additional 19.57 lakh jobs, which if again multiplied by five would benefit another 97.85 lakh SCs/STs. Even then about 17 crore would be left out, exemplifying the limits of reservations and also the limits of reservation-driven SC/ST movements (Ibid.: 57). Thus, the government sector has outlived its potential and educated Dalits must now look for other avenues.

Moving beyond
Protective Discrimination

While there is growing recognition of the need to move beyond state-led reservation policies and to devise new and innovative affirmative action policies to help Dalits—scholars and activists are divided over the type of strategies to be used. Since the late 1990s, two positions can be discerned in the existing literature: extension of the policy of reservation in employment to the private sector and the adoption of supplier diversity based on affirmative action.

Reservation in the Private Sector

A section of scholars and activists believe that extension of reservations to the private sector is urgently needed (Thorat *et al.* 2005). They point out that jobs in the government, including the public sector, are shrinking due to liberalization. Due to the emergence of a market economy, it is the private sector which is the fastest growing section of the economy today. While some feel that job reservation in the private sector could be voluntary and follow the American pattern of affirmative action, others demanding equal opportunity argue that legal sanctions are urgently required without which the policy, unlike in the US, will not be successful. The private sector, it is alleged, practices caste-based discrimination in its employment practices. They hold that this has been historically true in India and has continued through the colonial period to the present (Papola 2005).

A number of recent studies have tried to show that even in the relatively well-off segments of the formal, urban labour market, such as the IT sector, there is serious evidence of continued discriminatory barriers even for highly qualified Dalits. Thorat and Attewell provide the results of a field experiment that found that low caste applicants who are equally or better qualified than upper caste applicants, are significantly less likely to pass through hiring filters in the modern formal sector in India (Thorat and Attewell 2010). A similar study that carried out a qualitative, interview-based study of human resource managers responsible for hiring practices in 25 Indian firms suggests that this is because managers bring to the hiring process a set of stereotypes that makes it difficult for very low caste applicants to succeed in the competition for positions (Jodhka and Newman 2010). The experience of highly qualified Dalit students moving out of major universities into the job market show that they are far less likely to be hired due to preconceived notions among human resource managers of 'merit' (Deshpande and Newman 2010).

Based on their findings, such studies have argued that human capital differentials such as education, skills, and training alone cannot explain the lack of advancement of disadvantaged groups. Neither greater investment in education, nor the emergence of a more open, competitive market and a strong private sector with more jobs can correct this 'inefficiency in labour allocation' based on serious discrimination. Oliver Mendelsohn and Maria Vicziany have described the attitude of employers towards Dalits:

Given a choice, it would seem that employers [in private sector] will ordinarily opt for a caste Hindu over a Scheduled Caste person. It might be argued that the caste Hindu is likely to have a stronger record of academic achievement and greater social presence as a result of the usual disparity in family background. But it is highly doubtful that this is a sufficient explanation.

> There are now considerable numbers of Dalits who can compete equally with high-caste people for at least middle-level positions. Unless attitudes change, or unless reservation is extended to the private sector, the lack of a Dalit presence there will reinforce their lowly social position. (Mendelsohn and Vicziany 1998)

Accordingly, the need for a well-defined affirmative action policy for the private sector to fulfil its 'corporate social responsibility' has been raised. At present the private sector is completely free from any obligation toward minority businesses that suffer from discrimination and lack of capital (Thorat *et al.* 2005). Government provides a range of safeguards to the private sector to promote their business: tax concessions, supportive export-import policies, support from public sector banks, land at a cheap rate, better institutions for improving trade and industry. At the same time, uplifting of the SC/ST enshrined in the Constitution is the obligation of the government as well as the private sector. Hence, it has been argued by the supporters of this policy that if the private sector does not fulfil these obligations, legislation to make reservation in the private sector mandatory, is required.

However, the corporate sector in India has not responded favourably to the idea. Through its business chambers, it has made it clear that it is opposed to reservations and suppliership/dealerships based on legal sanctions (Jogdand 2005: 162). While the corporate sector could be adopting this position partly because of bias or prejudice against Dalits, this also stems from fears about affirmative action policies: return to the 'licence raj' State which would be costly, repressive, and counterproductive and result in loss of profit in a situation of rising global competition (Mehta 2005; Mitra 2005: 241). Rather, some sections are open to these practices provided they are on an informal and voluntary basis subject to merit. Federation of Indian Chambers of Commerce and Industry (FICCI) has also suggested that they are prepared to organize initiatives to increase employability and train Dalits, in skill and entrepreneurial development, to work for them and to set up their own businesses. A recent CII–Assocham Action Plan 2007, stressing on a cohesive and integrated society, in which all individuals have equal access to opportunities for personal growth (Action Plan 2007) commits industry to 'concrete steps' for greater inclusiveness for SC/STs in 'workplace, in business partnerships and in capacity building' (Ibid.).

Maharashtra is the only state that passed a legislation in 2001 under Article 348 of the Constitution making reservations mandatory in private institutions which receive aid from the government. Any local or statutory authority constituted under any Act of the state legislature; a cooperative society in which share capital is held by the government; government-aided institutions, including institutions or industries which have been given aid prior to the coming into force of this Act or, thereafter in the form of government land at concessional rates or other monetary concessions, and institutions that are recognized, licensed, supervised, or controlled by the government, come under its purview. This is the Maharashtra State Public Services (Reservation for Scheduled Castes, Scheduled Tribes, De-notified Tribes, Nomadic Tribes, Special Backward Category and other Backward Classes) Act, 2001. The only exceptions mentioned are super specialized posts in medical, technical, and educational fields; temporary appointments of less than 45 days; or single posts (isolated) in any cadre or grade. The principle of not giving such benefits to the 'creamy layer' as defined by the Social Justice and Cultural Affairs Department of the government, will apply to all categories mentioned above except for SC and ST; it is inter-transferable; effective at all stages of promotion and vacancies can be carried forward for up to five years in case of direct and up to three years in case of promotion. Non-compliance by an officer of the government or of the organization concerned carries a punishment of imprisonment for 90 days or a fine of Rs 5000, or both. The Act led to agitations in the Marathwada region specially Aurangabad and Latur and has made big industrialists belonging to the Confederation of Industry and IT industries unhappy. Some industrialists met the Chief Minister Sushil Kumar Shinde and they hinted at moving their industries out of Maharashtra. The Chief Minister in the discussions made it clear that the Act would be applicable to those industries and cooperatives with a 51 per cent share (Jogdand 2004). The state government has not made attempts to implement the legislation leaving Dalit activists unhappy.

Due to pressure for introducing reservations in the private sector, the United Progressive Alliance (UPA)-I Government based on the Common Minimum

Programme (CMP), set up a Group of Ministers to arrive at a workable policy. Inside parliament, R.S. Gavai submitted a non-official resolution in the Rajya Sabha on 16 April 2004. Some chief ministers have taken cognizance of the demand for this policy. S.M. Krishna while in office agreed that some form of private sector reservation was inevitable (Omvedt 2005). The BSP government in Uttar Pradesh following its victory in 2007 offered incentives to private entrepreneurs for setting up units in the state, if they provided 30 per cent reservation of jobs for people belonging to the SC, OBC, minorities and the 'economically backward upper castes'. The 30 per cent quota being sought was to be equally divided, with the SC, OBCs and minorities together, while the economically backward upper castes would get 10 per cent each. While the details were not clear, the incentives included concessions in stamp duty, relaxation in trade tax, excise rebate, and many other facilities. Industrialists interested in buying sick PSUs belonging to the State government would also get a loan waiver. Existing industrial units, service sector projects, and educational institutions could also avail of the incentives if they implemented the policy. The policy is purely voluntary and industrial units not interested in incentives could go ahead without implementing reservations (Kalhans 2007). However, industrialists in Uttar Pradesh have refused to consider the proposals.

Democratizing Capital through
Supplier Diversity (SD)

The second position, emerging from the authors and supporters of the BD, lays greater emphasis on the market mechanism and the need for 'democratization of capital' or broadening its ownership that would end the marginalization and exclusion of Dalits from industry and business. They hold that rather than reservation in the private sector—it is the business sector which holds the greatest promise in the years to come—with a large number of educated unemployed moving out of universities and colleges. The SD policy has features that borrow from both the Protective Discrimination (PD) policies of the past and from affirmative action: it is a state-supported policy implemented by the bureaucracy—but it is also a market-based voluntary policy, whose success depends upon the entrepreneurial skills and ability to supply goods and services in a time-bound manner in keeping with established standards. But there is continued caste–bias, competition, and even monopoly by the traditional suppliers to the government belonging largely to the upper or middle castes. Arguing that the market, technology, and skill development can play a decisive role—the BD demands that both the state and the private sector practise diversity policies such as giving dealerships and contracts to Dalits, together with other supportive measures such as provision of credit to bring them into the field of business and industry (BD 2002). This would create an entrepreneurial middle class from these communities which will bring them into the mainstream, make them part of economic decision–making, and give them a share in the fruits of development. It is also argued that such a policy will, in the long run, take the pressure off from reservations in higher education with more Dalits attracted to business and industry.

The advocates of the second position do not recommend doing away with reservations. They expect the government to implement the policy better and fill the entire backlog. But they point to the limitation of the 'emancipatory role' of these jobs (Prasad 2005:

167). Prasad argues that mere extension of this model, that is, of reservations into the private sector would not be of much use. He holds that at a conservative estimate—low-skilled, semi-skilled, and unskilled workers add up to more than three-fourths of the workforce of the private sector. Out of some 20 lakh white-collar jobs, the share of the SCs/STs through reservation would be about 5 lakh. Moreover, it remains to be seen if the private sector will calculate the backlog in these jobs—which are currently held by non-Dalit and non-tribals—and fill the vacancies. Even the government has not been able to do so till date. In terms of new appointments for Dalits in the private sector, he points out; the same will run into a few thousands at the best of times (Ibid.).

The advocates of the policy of SD draw on American affirmative action programmes that attempt to democratize capital and the more recent Black Economic Empowerment Programme in South Africa. The US programmes bring minorities into the area of business and industry by reserving for them fixed percentages in purchases by the federal government, in selection of government contractors where federal funds are involved, in providing credit requirements to underserved communities, and following non-discriminatory practices in employment. The authors of the BD drew on the US model because they wanted to put forward programmes which are voluntary and based on diversity, and therefore more suited to a liberalized economy different from the state-supported PD policies of the past. At the same time, the idea of the 'need to democratize capital' is drawn by scholars from India's unequal society and the resulting backwardness of Dalits. It is argued that so far, capital has remained the monopoly of a small and select group of individuals and families belonging mainly to the trading community (Markovits 2008; Tripathi 1984; Tripathi and Jumani 2007). Lower caste groups such as the Nadars in the Tamil region, Ramgarhias in Punjab, and the Mahishyas of Bengal perhaps constitute the few exceptions (Tripathi 1984). This must be the path of India's Dalits and tribals too. But they have not trodden it yet. A recent study by Harish Damodaran investigating the caste origins of many of India's industrialists found three main historical trends (Damodaran 2008: 315–16). First, is what he calls a 'bazaar to factory' route, the passage used by hereditary traders into industry. Second, a route from 'office to factory' that describes the recent movement of well-educated, high–caste Hindus, including Brahmins, into business. The third trajectory, from 'field to factory' has been the transition route into the business world of members of India's middle and lower peasant castes. This, Damodaran argues must be the path of India's Dalits and tribals too. But they have not trodden it yet; across India, Damodaran could not find a significant Dalit industrialist, not even in the south (Ibid.: 315); Similarly, a recent study which used information from the the Economic Census 1990, 1998, and 2004 pointed out substantial caste differ-ences in enterprises across the country: SCs and STs are under-represented in the ownership of enterprises and share of the work-force employed in them (Iyer and Varshney 2013).

The authors of the BD argue that Dalit entrepre-neurs can be created with state support if at present, the private sector is reluctant to participate in this policy. Pointing out that the Indian state has helped the industrial entrepreneur both during the period of protection and the era of globalization through various incentives such as lower taxes, land at conces-sional rates, etc., Prasad argues that Dalits will require state support as new entrepreneurs find it difficult to obtain a steady and assured market for their goods since breaking the monopoly held by established manufacturers or traders and obtaining financial stability is difficult. Government help in the form of a share in government contracts or supplies provides infant industries protection and the ability to repay loans and survive. Once established with support from the government, over time, a Dalit might gravitate to becoming an industrial entrepreneur selling in the open market as well (The Bhopal Document 2002).

State supported attempts could begin with SD policies in areas where little formal education or complex skills are required. Government departments buy a number of ordinary items such as stationery, furniture, office equipment, and electrical gadgets from suppliers in the market in bulk and also give dealerships for petrol, diesel, kerosene, and LPG, etc. If a percentage of these goods or supply contracts could be reserved, it would stimulate Dalit businesses, and over time such entrepreneurs could graduate to becoming manufacturers (Ibid.) The private sector, Prasad argues could start by outsourcing 5 or 10 per cent services to Dalits and making a conscious effort of integrating them in the supply chain (Ibid.). This would lead to much lower displacement than job reservations in the private sector, would not become an emotive issue, and there would be less social polarization. These ideas are supported by a growing cross-section of scholars who agree that rather than providing reservation in the private sector—which would yield only a meagre number of jobs—it is better to provide Dalits with a share in the ownership of private capital (Vaidyanathan, 2005; Weisskopf 2006: 718). There is need to provide share in business opportunities—worth crores—in public works, liquor licences, numerous broadcasting licences and so forth. These contracts, awarded by the central or state government, could create 'Dalit capitalists' (Sachar 2006). More recently, intellectuals and leaders from the Dalit middle class, some of whom were associated with the BD, have helped in the establishment of Dalit Indian Chamber of Commerce in Delhi and other cities. These individuals have argued that foreign direct investment (FDI) in retail would actually help Dalit entrepreneurs overcome the system of middlemen that exists in *mandi*s (agricultural markets) and emerge as businessmen. They argue that Dalits will succeed in occupations that are new and caste-neutral in origins rather than in traditional situations. The tools of modernity would help Dalits progress faster.

Madhya Pradesh, under the Digvijay Singh-led Congress was the first state in 2002 to adopt the policy of SD based on the BD to help Dalits enter the field of business and industry (Pai 2010). It can be described as a bold, new initiative or experiment for the uplift-ment of Dalits. Its adoption marked a shift in the rights and entitlements-based approach used to address Dalit concerns, to an approach which advocated a stake in the economy of the country. Although the policy was modelled on the US Government's provision of suppli-erships and dealerships to members of minority com-munities, the actual policies framed and implemented were in keeping with local requirements. More specifi-cally, under the policy of SD, two interrelated schemes were adopted: the 30 per cent scheme under which 30 per cent of all government supply orders were reserved for enterprises in which Dalits (and tribals) have a min-imum share of 50 per cent; and the Rani Durgawati Scheme (RDS) or margin money scheme to provide credit to Dalit/tribal entrepreneurs to encourage them to set up their own enterprises. Rules were carefully formulated at both the state and district level to help Dalits/tribals adopt supplierships or set up manufacturing units and wide publicity was given to encourage these groups to make use of the programme. Implemented by the SC/ST Welfare Department and coordinated by the Commerce and Industry Department, it was designed as a decentralized policy to be implemented by the District Trade and Industry Centres (DTICs) already functioning in each district of the state. They were given powers for special registration of Dalit/tribal entrepreneurs who wished to adopt the policy. Targets were set for each district, funds allotted, and an attempt made to promote the policy through widespread publicity in an attempt to reach out to educated unemployed youth in all parts of the state. The policies were implemented in August 2002 based on extensive rules and orders. The successor BJP government has continued these policies, though with some changes, and they have now become part of accepted government policy in Madhya Pradesh (Pai 2010).

A study using official data on adoption and spread of the SD policy, during the period of Congress rule, reveals that it was limited to a small Dalit class based mainly in the better off districts and cities and towns in the state such as Bhopal, Gwalior, Indore, Jhabua, etc. Considering that Dalits and tribals together constitute almost a quarter of the total population of Madhya Pradesh, the number that adopted the policy is as yet small. Moreover, the items being supplied were few and limited largely to stationery and government supplies—the number of Dalits who had taken to supply of more specialized goods or manufacturing under this policy were also few (Pai 2010). However, an in depth examination of nine selected Dalit entrepreneurs in Bhopal city shows that while none of them are large scale manufacturers, six have been able to successfully supply the contracted material and three are producers of the material they supply to government departments. Despite problems, some entrepreneurs in the sample have been fairly successful in their business venture and hope to do even better in the future. It has improved their socio-economic conditions substantially and they can be described as a vanguard that has set an example to others in the community to make similar efforts (Pai 2010). They represent a new class of young and educated Dalits to be found in many of the bigger cities of Madhya Pradesh, who have in recent

145

years moved from smaller towns and villages to Bhopal, and are prepared to take the risk of starting a business or industry. Dalit entrepreneurs in Madhya Pradesh have welcomed the SD policy and shown keenness to adopt it as it could provide them an opportunity to improve their socio-economic position. The study indicates that the SD policy is moving in a positive direction (Ibid.).

★ ★ ★

Middle class activism represents the third strand, together with movements and political parties—of the Dalit movement of India. An educated Dalit middle class has emerged in recent years, which has a different worldview regarding the role of the state, market, and civil society in the working of policies of protective discrimination, compared to an older generation of political leaders. In a period of globalization, it believes that all these agencies need to be involved in the creation and nurturing of an industrial/business middle class which would provide Dalits an important position within the economy. Based on this viewpoint, two new policies of affirmative action have been debated in recent years—particularly in the Bhopal Conference in 2002 that represented a significant gathering of educated Dalits: reservation in the private sector and supplier diversity to enable democratization of capital. While the former remains mired in controversy with the private sector not willing to accept legislation that would make reservations mandatory; the latter is lesser known and has been attempted only in Madhya Pradesh. At the same time, the BD has been forgotten since neither Congress nor any other political party has taken up these issues.

Both the policies discussed have many limitations due to which Dalits may not be able to gain full benefits. These would help only the educated and urban Dalits and have little to offer to the vast poor and illiterate majority, particularly in the backward states. Certain conditions are required if these policies are to benefit a larger number of Dalits—a sizeable educated class capable and willing to take entrepreneurial risks; a growing industrial sector that could provide opportunities to Dalits to become part of the supplier/dealer chain of the government or private sector; and a sympathetic political class and committed senior bureaucracy willing to help struggling entrepreneurs deal with corruption, caste bias, and monopoly practices of the traditional suppliers. In fact, the rise of middle class activism and the schemes it has put forward have created a divide among the better-off and poorer rural groups.

Despite these problems it can be argued that in the prevailing globalizing economy, the policy of SD has considerable latent possibilities for economic advancement and uplift of Dalits. Though a state-supported policy, it is at the same time voluntary, competitive, market-based, depends on individual ability, and is therefore less contentious or socially disruptive than land distribution or even reservations in the private sector given the opposition from the latter. As it is a voluntary policy, it might be easier to persuade the private sector also to adopt it. The policy has the prospect of making Dalits part of the supply chain and thereby bringing them into the business or industrial sector. In recent years Dalits have entered the political arena in large numbers, formed political parties and governments, but remain conspicuously absent in the business and industrial sector. Policies such as SD would end the marginalization and exclusion that these disadvantaged sectors face in the economic arena and provide them economic empowerment. It can be seen as a second stage in PD—a policy suited to the shift from a socialist welfare state to a neoliberal state—that is still expected in a democratic society to look after the welfare of the disadvantaged sections. It has the potential to introduce substantial change in the socio-economic position of Dalits, even though so far, the results in Madhya Pradesh have not matched the expectations voiced by Dalit intellectuals and activists when the programme was inaugurated.

Conclusion

Future Direction

On the basis of ideas presented, it is now possible to discuss the progress and achievements, limitations and weaknesses, and the future direction of the phenomenon of Dalit assertion and of the Dalit movement in the country. The process of questioning upper caste dominance began during the anti-colonial struggle when Dalits became aware of their lowly position and desired to overcome it—motivated by leaders such as Gandhi, Ambedkar, Periyar, and others—who attempted in various ways to address the issue of caste inequality. But as obtaining independence was the primary goal, the caste question assumed greater centrality only during post-Independence. The colonial period also witnessed the development of different ideological strands and identities in different regions—Gandhian, Ambedkarite, and Dravidian—that continued into the post-Independence period as part of the legacy of the anti-colonial struggles. However, these underwent considerable change after independence due to the new social and political context in which they had to function. The rise of Dalit assertion cannot be understood separate from the long term process of democratization, that is, the impact of both democracy and development after independence has to be accounted for. Our analysis suggests this is a multifaceted process influenced by a host of changes: adoption of adult franchise, land reforms, establishment of democratic institutions, rise in literacy, political consciousness, and emergence of lower caste identity. This process has been part of the larger transition from an elitist upper caste and class-based democracy at independence—to one which is gradually becoming more inclusive—as an ongoing process it will face many obstacles, resistance, and even violence.

Within this broader process, the construction of the identity of Dalit has been a major milestone in the progress of the Dalit movement in India. In contrast to earlier names such as Harijan and SC, the term Dalit arose from an upsurge from below, based a more radical ideology that stridently challenged Brahminism, upper caste domination, and oppression. The Gandhian strand played an important role in the immediate post-Independence period—but it was eclipsed by the 1980s by a strong wave of assertion from below in the Hindi heartland—which was critical of Gandhi and the Congress party and claimed the legacy of Dr Ambedkar. In Tamil Nadu too, since the 1980s, Dalits have moved away from Dravidian identity as they feel that the non-Brahmin and middle castes have not accorded them social equality and respect. In their search for an independent Dalit identity, they moved closer to Ambedkarism. Thus, over the last two decades, Ambedkar has emerged as the new icon for Dalits—his statues are found all over the country, his ideas underlie many movements and have also created a politics of symbolism.

However, Dalit identity suffers from internal differentiation which has not allowed the Dalit movement to move forward at a rapid and sustained pace after an initial radical surge in the 1980s and 1990s. Despite the fact that the word Dalit points to oppressive practices such as untouchability faced by the entire community, it has not been able to create a sense of togetherness and unity within the Dalit community. Right from the beginning, it carried different connotations for different groups: the Dalit Panthers defined it more inclusively in class terms including large sections of the underprivileged while parties and movements such as the BSP have viewed it in narrower, communitarian terms. It has been argued that the roots of such fragmentation lie in the existence of a hierarchical arrangement among Dalit sub-castes, below the line of pollution. Some sections of the urban and educated Dalit middle class also do not like the term as they feel it carries the baggage of historical suffering and wrongs perpetuated by the upper castes. Finally, the manner in which democratic politics has operated has been instrumental in creating greater competition between various sections of Dalits over contentious issues such as reservation and employment.

Thus Dalit identity in different regions and states has been different as it is the product of the specific social, economic, and political context, and the extent of democratization with little in common with similar struggles elsewhere. In Uttar Pradesh, the BSP was initially viewed as a Chamar party, however, due to successful mobilization the BSP has been able to consolidate the Dalit vote—though on the ground strong differences remain between the Chamars and Balmikis as before. In Tamil Nadu on the other hand, despite strong assertion, greater economic and educational advancement among Dalits—two separate political parties based on two specific sub-castes, the Pallars and Parayars have emerged—fragmenting the onslaught on upper and middle caste dominance. In Maharashtra too, divisions run deep among the Buddhist and Hindu Dalits and among the Mahars and other sections which has effectively divided the movement in the state. Nor were the Dalit Panthers, despite their ideological strength and writings, able to unite the Dalits.

Dalit assertion has over the last few decades translated into different modes of mobilization, movements, and organization, namely grass roots movements, political parties, and middle class activism. These are a product of democratic processes in the country to which Dalits have also been subject. The existence of three strands has arguably strengthened the Dalit movement as it has been able to respond to different types of challenges faced by Dalits in different situations: at the grass roots in everyday village life, in electoral politics, and more recently the challenge of liberalization, which has introduced marked changes in the economy. New forms of assertion have emerged that have attempted to deal with the rapid changes that are taking place in Indian democracy.

Movements at the grass roots today, constitute the most important form of Dalit assertion. It is at the village level that questioning of the caste hierarchy and confrontation between Dalits and backwards is the strongest. Movements at the grass roots were visible in the colonial period in regions such as western and southern India where organized anti-caste movements took place, prior to independence, demanding greater inclusiveness. Elsewhere such movements have been late or delayed and arose after independence, in most cases in the 1980s. Such movements are qualitatively different and reflect a deep disillusionment and anger with the failure of the post-Independence state to remove untouchability and protect the life and property of the Dalits against upper and middle caste atrocities. These movements are products of socio-political changes visible over the last few decades in the states: the emergence of a new and educated Dalit middle and lower middle class at the state and local level, rise in literacy and corresponding shift to non-agricultural occupations, economic improvement due to developments such as the Green Revolution, and avenues of non-agricultural employment—creating greater potential to revolt.

Grass roots movements have taken many different forms in different regions. Everywhere they have created new identities, alternative ideologies, and organizations in order to challenge upper and middle caste domination. They have had two main dimensions—economic and cultural. The former has questioned the feudal structure of the village based on control over land, wages, use of water sources, and traditional forms of occupations. These aspects are more important in backward states such as Uttar Pradesh, Madhya Pradesh, and Bihar where alternative sources of employment are not yet available to many Dalits and the landowning middle castes are capable of wielding considerable control over them. The cultural dimension has addressed issues of social inclusion such as the continued practice of untouchability, according respect and equal status involving freedom to use village roads, temple entry and participation, etc. These issues are more important in states such as Tamil Nadu where Dalits have achieved better education and employment and are demanding improved social status commensurate with their improved economic position.

However, this study indicates that in both developed and backward states, there is tremendous resistance to introducing change in the village power structure and in interpersonal relations between upper and lower castes. The position of the upper and middle castes has been seriously questioned, but Dalits face many forms of exclusion and are struggling to improve their social status. This explains the high levels of contestation and violence in panchayats and villages in many parts of the country. Even the existence of a Dalit government in Uttar Pradesh or a government of non-Brahmin backward caste groups in Tamil Nadu has not been able to prevent atrocities against Dalits. The use of the Scheduled Castes and Tribes (Prevention of Atrocities) Act 1989 by state governments has increased confrontation and violence against Dalits. A reason for rising violence is that Dalits are no longer prepared to put up with atrocities, as in the past, but fight back leading to prolonged confrontation which the state finds difficult to stem.

A major limitation of grass roots movements, which has not allowed their impact to be fully realized, is the increasing division among Dalit sub-castes, despite rising levels of political consciousness. It was expected that these divisions, which have their roots in the existence of a caste hierarchy below the line of pollution, would be overcome due to modernization, democratization, and political mobilization. However, paradoxically these processes have heightened identity consciousness leading to intense competition among various sub-castes for reservation and employment; examples being competition between the Chamars and Balmikis in Uttar Pradesh, Malas and Madigas in Andhra Pradesh, Mahars and Matangs in Maharashtra, etc. The result has been the weakening of the Dalit movement at the grass roots, where paradoxically today it is the strongest. Consequently, Dalits have not been able to effectively unite against oppression by the middle castes who are today their main oppressors. But, conflict is not always a negative feature; it often accompanies and is a symptom of change. The unequal caste hierarchy is being questioned and attempts are being made to dismantle it, this is being resisted by the middle and backward castes.

Dalit assertion and movements during the 1980s were initially non-political and critical of mainstream parties, which they described as casteist in composition and outlook. But within a decade, these radical movements transformed themselves into sectarian political parties—whose main aim has been to capture political power—though they remain movements as their main purpose remains to mobilize larger sections of Dalits into the political arena over time. However, with the institutionalization of Dalit movements into parties, they face challenges different from mainstream parties which make them prone to divisions and splits. Also frustrated over time with their inability to increase their narrow support base, they tend to form alliances with mainstream parties often leading to dilution of hard won identity.

There are undoubtedly definite advantages in forming political parties as it provides an immediate platform to mobilize against injustice and oppose various forms of oppression. For instance, the formation of a strong party such as the BSP has great symbolic value and created tremendous self-confidence among Dalits—particularly the poorer sections in the countryside. The spread of the power of the vote among

Dalit groups, which was earlier not possible, and the feeling of creating a 'Dalit government' has provided a sense of empowerment. In Tamil Nadu, it has enabled Dalits to successfully fight for civil rights and facilitated entry into the public sphere, denied in some areas even today. In Maharashtra, the presence of the RPI—despite its poor showing—kept right wing parties in check until recently. However, the constraining aspects cannot be denied. With the formation of parties, the long-term Dalit movement has lost considerable strength and vigour and electoral politics has occupied centre-stage. In Uttar Pradesh, the BSP formed coalition governments with the BJP—an upper caste right wing party—and despite efforts by the BSP leadership, had to compromise on many issues. It also led the party leadership to take increasingly softer stands vis-à-vis the upper castes, with a view to widen its social base and gain power—culminating in the adoption of the policy of Sarvajan in the first decade of the twenty-first century. Critics have argued that the defeat of the party in the 2012 elections was due to unhappiness among Dalits—including the Chamars who form its core constituency—over granting of numerous benefits to the Brahmins. Mayawati made concerted efforts to win back the confidence of the Dalits but in the process lost the support of the upper castes and the BSP was defeated in the 2012 assembly elections.

Similarly Dalit organizations in Tamil Nadu, many with a radical Marxist bent, initially moved away from Dravidian identity to pursue an autonomous grass roots struggle, against rising middle and backward caste domination and oppression. This created a period of intense confrontation between the two sides, evidenced in the caste riots in the late 1990s in the southern districts. However, many of these organizations have joined hands to create two major political parties—the DPI and the PT and also formed pre-electoral alliances with both Dravidian parties, the DMK and the AIADMK. Their attempt to form an independent Dalit identity by adopting Ambedkarism did not meet with much success—Periyar, a major Dravidian leader, still remains an icon among them. This raises the question of who is a Dravidian today: only non-Brahmins or, is it inclusive of Dalits and Brahmins also, making it an identity based on region and language, but not caste. Such developments signal the dilution of Dravidian identity, and in this situation, Dalits in Tamil Nadu have not been able to resolve the issue of their self-identity.

Another difficulty is that in Tamil Nadu, Dalit parties are based on sub-castes and therefore do not get the support of all sections of the Dalits. Electoral politics, rather than uniting sub-castes on a common platform against mainstream parties, has created further divisions and even violence among sub-castes—and resulted in further weakening of the Dalit movement in Tamil Nadu—allowing the middle and backward castes particularly the Thevars and Gounders, to dominate and oppress the Dalits. The impact of this has been felt on elections at the state and panchayat level, where Dalits have attempted to make their presence felt. Caste politics has in fact determined the shape of the party system; in the 1960s Tamil Nadu had a neat two party system in which the Congress, and the DMK—a product of the non-Brahmin movement—competed for power. Today, the party system is fragmented due to the splintering of the DMK into a number of Dravidian parties, and on the other, the rise of many small Dalit parties which has greatly weakened the Congress and the Left parties in the state.

In more recent years, Dalit assertion has taken a different turn with the rise of Dalit middle class activism. This activism is the result of a tiny but influential

Dalit class which is better educated and a product of both democratization and globalization in the 1990s. As beneficiaries of 60 years of protective discrimination and state welfare, the hopes, aspirations, and vision of the future held by this class is different. Not attracted to assertion and political mobilization through movements and parties, which they feel creates confrontation and violence, they stress on the urgent need for economic empowerment. They strongly argue that Indian society cannot become a genuine democracy without reforming both its traditional institutions and creating new ones suited to the present-day context. They also highlight a tension between the democratic norms adopted in the Constitution and the continued existence of a casteist society, and hold that a new societal consensus is required between the upper and lower castes. Based on this middle class ideology, this class argues that Dalits must be integrated into the Indian polity, society, and economy at a better level than has been happening so far. Critical of the existing policy of protective discrimination, the Dalit middle class feels that while it may have served the purpose so far—fresh and innovative policies suited to a new social and political context are required, otherwise

Dalits will continue to occupy lowly positions in the society and economy. This newly mobile Dalit middle class of entrepreneurs and professionals would like to assume leadership and be the vanguard for the poorer sections of the Dalit community. Two new policies have been suggested: reservation in the private sector and supplier diversity, which it is felt, will not create confrontation since these do not involve mobilization and competition with other sections and Dalit individuals will obtain upward mobility and improvement in their economic status.

However, it is questionable whether the middle class thrust has blunted the radical edge of assertion at the grass roots and in electoral politics—or are these separate processes each impacting different sections of Dalits. It is also true that these new policies are narrowly constructed, meant only for the better-off, educated, and urban Dalit middle class which still constitutes a miniscule percentage of the community. These policies have nothing to offer to the large majority which remains poor, rural-based, and in sore need of education. Policies, such as job reservation in the private sector and supplier diversity, can be of use to Dalits, if access to good quality education at the school and university level were available to all sections—and not merely the elite sections among them. Theories of market discrimination also argue that disadvantaged groups which have little knowledge and experience of the workings of the market require considerable state support and entrepreneurial training to succeed in this field. The experience of reservation policy so far has been the creation of a small, privileged, bourgeois class and such policies deepen this trend. While Dalits should also enter areas of high technology, business, industry, and other better paying sectors of the economy—it is also necessary to simultaneously introduce policies to bridge the gap between those who can enter these fields, and others who remain trapped in older and often traditional occupations. So far, the benefits of reservation have been narrowly distributed to a small section and have contributed to the existing class inequalities in society. This has further divided the better-off sections from the poorer and marginalized sub-castes who feel left out and contribute to the rising demands for quotas for these groups. It is also the cause for the divide within the Dalit movement in better-off states such as Maharashtra, Karnataka, and Tamil Nadu where a small Dalit class has done well and has little in common with the large majority. Globalization, while it has much to offer to the educated among Dalits and non-Dalits, has had a differential impact, increasing caste and class inequalities.

A key question that emerges from the above discussion is: given the rising levels of Dalit assertion, can there be a single all-India Dalit ideology, movement or party in the future? Gail Omvedt, writing in the 1990s, evoked alternative 'Dalit visions' that could spread across the country (Omvedt 1995). Some examined features of Dalit assertion seem to support this idea: the process of democratization that is gradually covering all parts of the country, the formation of the identity of Dalit, and the emergence of Ambedkar as an icon of the Dalit movement everywhere. Another significant development in recent years has been of the rising tide of aspirations across the country of an emerging, young, educated, and politically aware class of Dalits with high ambitions. This is seen in the demand for reservation of jobs in the private sector so that Dalits can share in the fruits of liberalization, expectations that the central government will introduce diversity policies, and the establishment of Dalit chambers of commerce in a bid to create Dalit entrepreneurs.

However, the impact of the process of democratization has been uneven across the Indian subcontinent: rapid in some regions and slow in others with significant consequences for the Dalit movement. The large size and cultural diversity of the subcontinent, historically divergent patterns of colonial investment, different types of movements against caste oppression, and methods of mobilization and leadership created different legacies in the various regions. Dalit identity, despite according strength to movements against caste oppression, has different features and meanings and functions differently in different regions. It has not been a uniting force for Dalit leaders, movements, and parties. Despite the convergence of many movements and parties towards the ideas of Ambedkar, our study reveals that no all-India Dalit ideology or movement has developed. Thus while everywhere the problems faced by Dalits are similar, in each region or state the Dalit movement has developed along its own trajectory with distinct features and forms. In sum, the Dalit movement reflects the historical, regional, sociocultural, and increasing political diversity of the subcontinent.

More importantly, in recent years, the relationship between the processes of democratization and Dalit assertion has undergone change. On the one hand, democratization has been slow in spreading to new areas in the country. On the other hand, Dalit movements have undergone a process of institutionalization into political parties and organized middle class politics. As a consequence, the movement downwards of democratization and the accompanying process of Dalit assertion touching the poorer Dalit sub-castes, gradually including and empowering them, has slowed down. The new educated Dalit middle class is also far removed in its thinking and actions from the poorer sections and has distanced itself from grass roots activism, Dalit political parties, and their leadership. The attempt to build alliances between the Left and the Dalit movement has not been tried on a sustained basis and not yielded much success.

In this scenario, the real problem lies not in the lack of an all-India Dalit identity or movement. Despite a strong wave of assertion in many parts of the country and the many developments discussed, weaknesses remain that need to be overcome if the Dalit movement is to move forward and achieve its goal of greater social equality. These weaknesses lie partly within the Dalit community itself, and partly in the manner in which the processes of democracy and development have unfolded on the Indian subcontinent, since the colonial period. In the case of the former, unevenness in mobilization and spread of the Dalit movement; disunity and existence of fragmentation among Dalit sub-castes, and lack of leadership within the Dalit community have been the main obstacles. In the case of the latter, deprivation, poverty, and lack of educational and employment opportunities have affected Dalits, who constitute some of the most disadvantaged sections in the country.

In this situation, what is the future direction of the Dalit movement in the country? While the long term prognosis arising from our study is positive—many problems need to be addressed in the period of transition. Dalit assertion, and movements based on it, have been a part of our democratic system experience and cannot be understood apart from it. But has it really been a truly democratizing or empowering experience for the vast number of subaltern Dalits? So far, India has had a procedural democracy in which certain norms and institutions established at independence have been accepted. What is needed is a more substantial democracy in which there is not merely acceptance of the norms of equality and social justice, but actual implementation and practice, leading to a society of equal citizens without oppression and domination. Attempts are required to introduce changes that are truly anti-caste and attempt to transform the entire system. For this, two changes are needed: greater democratization that moves downwards and benefits the poorer and backward sections in all parts of the country, together with acceptance of this process, and change in attitude on the part of the upper and middle castes, leading to greater social equality. A second contributory requirement is more inclusive economic growth and greater equalization of educational and employment opportunities for Dalits which would also go a long way in removing competition and conflict between Dalit sub-castes, strengthening the Dalit movement. This would lead to an egalitarian society which was the vision at independence of the makers of the Indian Constitution.

References

Introduction: Dalit Assertion, Democratization, and Politics

Gorringe, H. 2005. *Untouchable Citizens, Dalit Movements and Democratisation in Tamil Nadu*. New Delhi: Sage Publications.

————. 2010. 'The Party Political Panthers: Electoral Politics & Social Change in Tamil Nadu', paper presented at the seminar on 'Dalits in Neo-Liberal India', Oxford University, 1–2 September.

Gupta, S.K. 1985. *The Schedule Castes in Modern Indian Politics Their Emergence as a Modern Power.* New Delhi: Manohar Publishers.

Guru, G. (ed.) 2009. *Humiliation Claims and Context.* New Delhi: Oxford University Press.

Huntington, S. 1991. *The Third Wave: Democratization in the Late Twentieth Century.* Norman and London: University of Oklahoma Press.

Jenkins, C.J. and B. Klandermans. (eds). 1995. *The Politics of Social Protest: Comparative Perspectives on States and Social Movements*. Minneapolis, MN: University of Minnesota Press.

Lipset, M. 1994. 'The Social Requisites of Democracy Revisited,' *American Sociological Review*, 59: 1–2.

Moore, B. 1996. *Social Origins of Dictatorship and Democracy: Lord and Master in the Making of the Modern World*. Boston: Boston Press.

Offe, C. 1990. 'Reflections on the Institutional Self-transformation of Movement Politics,' in R. Dalton and M. Kuechler (eds), *Challenging the Political Order*. Cambridge Polity Press, pp. 230–50.

Pai, S. 2002. *Dalit Assertion and the Unfinished Democratic Revolution: The BSP in Uttar Pradesh*. New Delhi: Sage Publications.

——————. 2000. *State Politics New Dimensions: Party System, Liberalization and Politics of Identity*. New Delhi: Shipra Publications.

Patnaik, U. and P. Patnaik. 2001. 'The State, Poverty and Development in India' in *Democratic Governance in India: Challenges of Poverty, Development and Identity*, pp. 32–64, New Delhi: Sage Publications.

Potter, D., D. Goldblatt, M. Kiloh, and P. Lewis. 1997. *Democratization*. USA: Polity Press.

Rueschmeyer, D., E. Stephens, and J. Stephens. 1992. *Capitalist Development and Democracy*. Cambridge: Cambridge University Press.

Rustow, W.W. 1970. 'Transitions to Democracy: Towards a Dynamic Model', *Comparative Politics*, 2(April): 337–63.

Salim, L. and P. Taneja. 2009. 'Balancing Democracy and Globalization in an Era of Coalition Politics: The Indian Experience', *South Asia: Journal of South Asian Studies*, 32: 3.

Shah, G. 2001. 'Dalit Politics: Has It Reached an Impasse?' in *Democratic Governance in India: Challenges of Poverty, Development and Identity.* New Delhi: Sage Publications.

Shah, G. 2000. *Social Movements in India: A Review of Literature,* New Delhi: Sage Publications.

Tarrow, Sidney. 1998. *Power in Movement. Cambridge:* Cambridge University Press.

Webster, J. 1995. 'Towards Understanding the Modern Dalit Movement', unpublished Ambedkar Lecture, Centre for the Study of Social Systems, Jawaharlal Nehru University, New Delhi.

Chapter 1

Crawley, W.F. 1971. 'Kisan Sabhas and Agrarian Revolt in the United Provinces 1920–21', *Modern Asian Studies*, 5(2):95–105.

Geetha, V. and S.V. Rajadurai. 1993. 'Dalits and Non-Brahmin Consciousness in Colonial Tamil Nadu', *Economic and Political Weekly*, 28(39): 2091–8.

Gore M.S. 1993. *Social Context of an Ideology: Ambedkar's Political and Social Thought.* Delhi: Sage Publications.

Gupta, S.K. 1985. *The Schedule Castes in Modern Indian Politics Their Emergence As a Modern Power.* New Delhi: Manohar Publishers.

Guru, G. 2010. 'Social Justice', in N.G. Jayal and B.P. Mehta (eds), *The Oxford Companion to Politics in India*, pp. 361–80, New Delhi: Oxford University Press.

Hardgrave, R.L. 1969. *The Dravidian Movement.* Bombay: Popular Prakashan.

Irschick, E. 1969. *Politics and Social Conflict in South India: The Non-Brahmin Movement and Tamil Separatism.* Berkeley: University of California Press.

Jurgensmeyer, M. 1988. *Religious Rebels in the Punjab: The Social Vision of Untouchables.* Delhi: Ajanta Publications.

Kshirsagar, R.K. 1994. *Dalit Movement in India and Its Leaders 1857–1956.* New Delhi: MD Publications.

Kumar, M. 1994. 'Caste and Political Mobilization in Tamil Nadu: A Study of the PMK', unpublished MPhil Thesis, Centre for Political Studies, Jawaharlal Nehru University, New Delhi.

Narayan, B. 2010. *Making of the 'Dalit Public' in North India: Uttar Pradesh 1950 to the Present.* New Delhi: Oxford University Press.

Neale, W. 1962. *Economic Change in Rural India Land Tenure and Reform in UP 1800–1955.* Yale: Yale University Press.

O'Hanlon, R. 1985. *Caste Conflict and Ideology: Mahatma Phule and Lower Caste Protest in the Nineteenth Century.* Cambridge: Cambridge University Press.

O'Hanlon, R. 2002. *Dalit Assertion and the Unfinished Democratic Revolution: the BSP in Uttar Pradesh*. New Delhi: Sage Publications.

Pai, S. 2007. 'From Dalit to Savarna: The Search for a New Social Constituency by the Bahujan Samaj Party in Uttar Pradesh', in S. Pai (ed.), *Political Process in Uttar Pradesh: Identity, Economic Reform and Governance*, pp. 221–40, New Delhi: Pearson.

—————. 2000. *State Politics New Dimensions: Party System, Liberalization and Politics of Identity*. New Delhi: Shipra Publications.

Pandey, G. 1978. *The Ascendancy of the Congress in UP 1926–34: A Study in Imperfect Mobilisation*. New Delhi: Oxford University Press.

Pandian, J. 1987. *Caste Nationalism and Ethnicity: An Interpretation of Tamil Cultural History and Social Order*. Bombay: Popular Prakashan.

Pandian, M.S.S. 1994(b). 'Notes on the Transformation of Dravidian Identity Tamil Nadu c. 1900–1940', Working Paper no. 120. Madras: Madras Institute of Development Studies.

Ram, R. 2008. 'Ravidas Dera and Social Protest: Making Sense of Dalit Consciousness in the Punjab', *Journal of Asian Studies,* 67(4).

Sachar, R. 2006. 'Towards Dalit Capitalism', *The Times of India*, 12 July, New Delhi.

Verma, A.K. 2012. 'Why Did Mayawati Lose?' *Economic and Political Weekly*, 47(18): 17–19.

Wiser and Wiser. 2001. *Behind Mud Walls: Seventy-five Years in a North Indian Village*. California: University of California Press.

Zelliot, E. 1979. 'Learning the Use of Political Means: The Mahars of Maharashtra' in R. Kothari (ed.), *Caste in Indian Politics,* pp. 29–69. New Delhi: Orient Longman.

Chapter 2

Anandhi, S. 2011. 'Beyond the Coherence of Identities: A Reading of Sedal', *Economic and Political Weekly* October 15, 46(42): 27–31.

Bhattacharya, S. 2003. 'Caste, Class and Politics in West Bengal: A Case Study of a Village in Burdwan', *Economic and Political Weekly*, January 18–24, 38(3): 242–6.

Byapari, M. 2007. 'Is There any Dalit Writing in Bangla?' *Economic and Political Weekly*, October 10, (42) 41: 4116–120.

Delige, R. 1977. *The World of the Untouchable Paraiyars*. New Delhi: Oxford University Press.

Duncan, I.R. 1979. 'Levels, the Communication of Programmes and Sectional Strategies in Indian Politics, with Reference to the BKD and the RPI in UP State and Aligarh District', unpublished thesis, University of Sussex.

Ganguly-Scrase, R. 2001. *Global Issues, Local Contexts: The Rabi Das of West Bengal*. Hyderabad: Orient Longman.

Gorringe, H. 2005. *Untouchable Citizens, Dalit Movements and Democratisation in Tamil Nadu*. New Delhi: Sage Publications.

Jaffrelot, C. 2003. *India's Silent Revolution: The Rise of the Low Castes in North Indian Politics*. New Delhi: Permanent Black.

Jaoul, N. 2007. 'Dalit Empowerment, "Non-political" Ambedkarites and the BSP: A Division of Political Labour?' in S. Pai (ed.), *Political Process in Uttar Pradesh: Identity, Economic Reform and Governance*, pp. 191–220, New Delhi: Pearson.

Jodhka, S.S. 2010. 'Caste and Power in the Lands of Agriculture: Revisiting Rural North West India', paper presented in the seminar on 'Mobility or Marginalization: Dalits in Neo-Liberal India', Oxford University, 1–2 September.

Jodhka, S.S. and Kumar, A. 2010. 'Religious Mobilizations for Development and Social Change: A Comparative Study of Dalit Movements in Punjab and Maharashtra, India' Working Paper no. 47. UK: University of Birmingham.

Jurgensmeyer, M. 1988. *Religious Rebels in the Punjab: The Social Vision of Untouchables*. Delhi: Ajanta Publications.

Kumar, A. 2012. 'Fallacy of the State in Bihar', *Economic and Political Weekly*, 47(44): 23–5.

Lynch, O. 1969. *The Politics of Untouchability: Social Mobility and Social Change in a City of India*. New York: Columbia University Press.

Malik, S.K. 2011. 'Dalit Protest and Temple Entry Movements in Orissa: A Study of Kendrapara District', unpublished MPhil thesis. New Delhi: Jawaharlal Nehru University.

Manikumar, K.A. 1997. 'Caste Clashes in Southern Tamil Nadu', *Economic and Political Weekly*, September 6, 32(36): 2242–3.

Mendelsohn, O. 1993. 'The Transformation of Authority in Rural India', *Modern Asian Studies,* 27(4): 804–42.

Moses, B.C. 1995 'Struggle for Panchamma Lands Dalit Assertion in Tamil Nadu', *Economic and Political Weekly*, February 4–10, 30(5): 247–8.

Narayan, B. 2010. *Making of the 'Dalit Public' in North India: Uttar Pradesh 1950 to the Present.* New Delhi: Oxford University Press.

Pai, S. 2000a. 'New Social and Political Movements of Dalits: A Study of Meerut District', *Contributions to Indian Sociology*, 2(34): 189–220.

————. 2002. *Dalit Assertion and the Unfinished Democratic Revolution: the BSP in Uttar Pradesh.* New Delhi: Sage Publications.

————. 2006. 'Dalit Reservation in a Hierarchical Society: Dialectics of Social Change', paper presented at the S.K. Dey Centennial Seminar on 'Deepening of Democracy through Democratic Decentralization: Challenges and Prospects', Institute of Social Sciences. New Delhi, 13 September.

Pai, S. 2010. 'Affirmative Action, Group Rights and Democracy: the Mala–Madiga Conflict in Andhra Pradesh' in Kumar, A. (ed.) *Rethinking State Politics in India: Regions within Regions,* New Delhi: Routledge.

Pandian, M.S.S. 2000. 'Dalit Assertion in Tamil Nadu: An Exploratory Note', *Journal of Indian School of Political Economy*, 12(3–4): 501–18.

Parthasarthi, M. 2011. 'Paramkudi Violence: Against Dalits, Against Politics', *Economic and Political Weekly*, 46(44–5): 14–17.

Rajangam, S. 2011. 'Rise of Dalit Movements and the Reaction of Dravidian Parties', in K. Satyanarayana and S. Tharu (eds), *No Alphabet in Sigh: New Dalit Writing from South India*, Dossier 1: Tamil and Malayalam. New Delhi: Penguin.

Satyanarayana and S. Tharu (ed.) 2011. *No Alphabet in Sight: New Dalit Writing from South India*. New Delhi: Penguin.

Shah G., H. Mander, S. Thorat, S. Deshpande, and A. Baviskar. 2006. *Untouchability in Rural India*. New Delhi: Sage Publications.

Singh, J. 1998. 'Ambedkarisation and Assertion of Dalit Identity: Socio-Cultural Protest in Meerut District of Western Uttar Pradesh', *Economic and Political Weekly*, 32(4): 2611–18. *Sociological Review* 59: 1–22.

Srinivasulu, K. 2011. 'A Valuable Intellectual Resource on Dalit Writing', *Economic and Political Weekly,* 46(36): 30–3.

Thirumaavalvan, R. 2003. *Talisman Extreme Emotions of Dalit Liberation*. New Delhi: Thirumaavalvan Samya Publications.

Chapter 3

Brass, P.R. 1968. 'Uttar Pradesh', in M. Weiner (ed.), *State Politics in India*, pp. 60–125. New Jersey: Princeton University Press.

Borpujari, P. 2013. '*A Film with a Difference*' accessed from Internet.

Contursi, J.A. 1993. 'Political Theology: Text and Practice in a Dalit Panther Community', *Journal of Asian Studies*, 52: 302–39.

Duncan, I.R. 1979. 'Levels, the Communication of Programmes and Sectional Strategies in Indian Politics, with reference to the BKD and the RPI in UP state and Aligarh District', Unpublished thesis, University of Sussex.

Geetha, V. and S.V. Rajadurai. 1993. 'Dalits and Non–Brahmin Consciousness in Colonial Tamil Nadu'. *Economic and Political Weekly* 28(39): 2091–8.

Gokhale, 1990. 'The Evolution of a Counter Ideology: Dalit Consciousness in Maharashtra', in M.S.A. Rao and Francine (eds), *Dominance and State Power in Modern India Decline of a Social Order,* II: 212-77, New Delhi: Oxford University Press.

Gokhale-Turner, J.B. 1979. 'The Dalit Panthers and the Radicalisation of Untouchables', *Journal of Commonwealth and Comparative Politics,* 28(1).

Gorringe, H. 2005. *Untouchable Citizens, Dalit Movements and Democratisation in Tamil Nadu.* New Delhi: Sage Publications.

Guru, G. 1994. 'Understanding Violence Against Dalits in Marathwada', *Economic and Political Weekly,* 29(9): 469–72.

Jeyaranjan, J. and S. Anandhi. 1999. 'New Caste Equations: Tamil Nadu', *Economic and Political Weekly,* January 9, 34(1–2): 15–16.

Karthikeyan, D., 2009. 'Tamil Nadu's Dalit Vote', *The Hindu,* 12 May.

Kartikeyan D., S. Rajangam, and H. Gorringe. 2012. 'Dalit Political Imagination and Replication in Contemporary Tamil Nadu', *Economic and Political Weekly,* September 8, 47(36): 30–3.

Kumar, A. 2004. 'A Comparative Study of the Black Panthers and the Dalit Panthers', unpublished PhD thesis. New Delhi: Jawaharlal Nehru University.

Kumar, P. 1999. 'Dalits and the BSP in UP Issues and Challenges', *Economic and Political Weekly,* 34(14): 822–6.

Morkhandikar, R.S. 1990. 'Dilemmas of the Dalit Movement in Mahrashtra: Unity Moves and After', *Economic and Political Weekly, March* 24–30, 25(12): 586–91.

Murugkar, L. 1991. *Dalit Panther Movement in Maharashtra: A Sociological Appraisal,* New Delhi: South Asia Books.

Narayan, B. 2006. *Women Heroes and Dalit Assertion in North India: Culture Identity and Politics.* New Delhi: Sage Publications.

Natrajan, B. 2013 'Punctuated Solidarities: Caste and Left Politics', *Economic and Political Weekly*, 48(6): 16–19.

Omvedt G. 1995. *Dalit Visions: The Anti-Caste Movement and the Construction of an India Identity*, pp. 1–6, New Delhi: Orient Longman.

——————. 2003. 'Introduction' in R. Thirumaavalvan (ed.), *Talisman Extreme Emotions of Dalit Liberation.* New Delhi: Samya Publications.

Pai, S. 2002. *Dalit Assertion and the Unfinished Democratic Revolution: the BSP in Uttar Pradesh*, pp. 1–6. New Delhi: Sage Publications.

——————. 2007. 'From Dalit to Savarna: The Search for a New Social Constituency by the Bahujan Samaj Party in Uttar Pradesh' in S. Pai (ed.), *Political Process in Uttar Pradesh: Identity, Economic Reform and Governance.* New Delhi: Pearson.

——————. 2009. 'The New Politics of Mayawati: Implications for State and National Politics', in V. Ramakrishnan (ed.), *Uttar Pradesh: The Road Ahead.* New Delhi: Academic Foundation.

Pandian, M.S.S. 1994. 'Crisis in the DMK', *Economic and Political Weekly*, January 29–February 4, 29(5): 221–3.

Singh S. 2010. 'Three Years of the BSP Government in UP', *Economic and Political Weekly*, 45(38): 77–81.

Thirumaavalvan, R. 2003. *Talisman Extreme Emotions of Dalit Liberation*, New Delhi: Samya Publications.

Verma, A.K. 2012. 'Why Did Mayawati Lose?' *Economic and Political Weekly*, 47(18).

Wyatt, A. 2009. *Party System Change in South India: Political Entrepreneurs, Patterns and Process*, London and New York: Routledge.

Chapter 4

Babu, S. 2003. 'Dalits and the New Economic Order: Some Prognostications and Prescriptions from the Bhopal Conference', RGICS Working Paper Series 44, New Delhi: Rajiv Gandhi Institute for Contemporary Studies.

Claude, M. 2008. '*Merchants, Traders, Entrepreneurs: Indian Business in the Colonial Era*. New Delhi: Permanent Black.

Damodaran, H. 2008. *India's New Capitalists: Caste, Business and Industry in a Modern Nation-State*, New Delhi: Permanent Black and The New India Foundation.

Deshpande, A. and K.S. Newman. 2010. 'Where the Path Leads: The Role of Caste in Post-University Employment Expectations' in S. Thorat and K.S. Newman (eds), *Blocked by Caste Economic Discrimination in Modern India*, pp. 88–122. New Delhi: Oxford University Press.

Fernandes, L. 2007. *India's New Middle Class Democratic Politics in an Era of Economic Reform*. New Delhi: Oxford University Press.

Iyer, L., and A. Varshney. 2013. 'Caste and Entrepreneurship in India', *Economic and Political Weekly*, 48(6): 52–60.

Jodhka, S.S. and K.S. Newman. 2010. 'In the Name of Globalization: Meritocracy, Productivity and the Hidden Language of Caste', in S. Thorat and K.S. Newman (eds), *Blocked by Caste Economic Discrimination in Modern India*, pp. 52–87. New Delhi: Oxford University Press.

Jogdand, P.G. 2005 'Reservation in the Private Sector Legislation in Maharashtra', in S. Thorat, Aryama, and P. Negi (eds), *Reservation and the Private Sector Quest For Equal Opportunity and Growth*, pp. 160–66. New Delhi: Rawat Publications with Indian Institute of Dalit Studies.

Kalhans, S. 2007. 'Mayawati Has New Proposal: Socio-Economic Engineering', *The Indian Express*, Delhi edn, 11 August.

Kapur, D., C.B. Prasad, L. Pritchett, and D.S. Babu. 2010. 'Rethinking Inequality: Dalits in Uttar Pradesh in the Market Reform Era', *Economic and Political Weekly* 45(35): 39–49.

Markovits, C. 2008. *Merchants, Traders, Entrepreneurs: Indian Business in the Colonial Era*. New Delhi: Permanent Black.

Mehta, B.P. 2005. 'New Agenda for Dalits', in S. Thorat, Aryama, and P. Negi (eds), *Reservation in Private Sector Quest for Equal Opportunity and Growth*, pp. 267–72. New Delhi: Rawat Publications with Indian Institute of Dalit Studies.

Mendelsohn, O. and M. Vicziany. 1998. *The Untouchables: Subordination, Poverty and the State in India.* Cambridge: Cambridge University Press.

Mitra, A. 2005. 'Is Reservation in the Private Sector Warranted?' in S. Thorat, Aryama, and P. Negi (eds), *Reservation and the Private Sector Quest For Equal Opportunity and Growth*, pp. 239–41. New Delhi: Rawat Publications with Indian Institute of Dalit Studies.

Nigam, A. 2002. 'In Search of a Bourgeoisie: Dalit Politics Enters a New Phase', *Economic and Political Weekly*, 37(13): 1190–3.

Omvedt G. 2005. 'Mythologies of Merit', in S. Thorat, Aryama and P. Negi (eds), *Reservation and the Private Sector Quest For Equal Opportunity and Growth,* pp. 202–6. New Delhi: Rawat Publications with Indian Institute of Dalit Studies.

Pandey, G. 2009. 'Can There Be a Subaltern Middle Class?' *Public Culture*, 21: 321–42.

Pai, S. 2010. 'Affirmative Action, Group Rights and Democracy: The Mala–Madiga Conflict in Andhra Pradesh,' in A. Kumar (ed.), *Rethinking State Politics in India: Regions within Regions*, New Delhi: Routledge.

―――――. 2010a. 'Dalit Entrepreneurs, Globalization and the Supplier Diversity Experiment in Madhya Pradesh, paper presented in the seminar on 'Mobility or Marginalization: Dalits in Neo-Liberal India, Oxford University, 1–2 September.

Pai, S. 2010b. *Developmental State and the Dalit Question in Madhya Pradesh: Congress Response*. New Delhi: Routledge.

Papola T.S. 2005. 'Social Exclusion and Discrimination in Hiring Practices: The Case of Indian Industry', in S. Thorat, Aryama, and P. Negi (eds), *Reservation and the Private Sector: Quest For Equal Opportunity and Growth*, pp. 101–8. New Delhi: Rawat Publications with Indian Institute of Dalit Studies.

Sachar, R. 2006. 'Towards Dalit Capitalism', *The Times of India*, New Delhi, July 12.

The Bhopal Document. 2002. *The Dalit Agenda Charting a New Course for Dalits for the 21st Century*. Bhopal: Government of Madhya Pradesh.

Thorat, S., Aryama, and P. Negi (eds). 2005. *Reservation and the Private Sector Quest for Equal Opportunity and Growth*. New Delhi: Rawat Publications with Indian Institute of Dalit Studies.

Thorat, S. and P. Attewell. 2010. 'The Legacy of Social Exclusion: A Correspondence Study of Job Discrimination in India's Urban Private Sector', in S. Thorat and K.S. Newman (eds), *Blocked by Caste Economic Discrimination in Modern India*, pp. 35–51. New Delhi: Oxford University Press.

Tripathi, D. (ed.). 1984. *Business Communities of India: A Historical Perspective*. New Delhi: Manohar Publishers.

Tripathi, D. and J. Jumani. 2007. *The Concise Oxford History of Indian Business*. New Delhi: Oxford University Press.

Vaidyanathan, R. 2005. 'Make Them Entrepreneurs Instead', in S. Thorat, Aryama, and P. Negi (eds), *Reservation and the Private Sector Quest for Equal Opportunity and Growth*, pp. 356–60. New Delhi: Rawat Publications with Indian Institute of Dalit Studies.

Weisskopf, T. 2006. 'Is Positive Discrimination a Good Way to Aid Disadvantaged Ethnic Communities', *Economic and Political Weekly*, February 25, 41(8): 1–23.

Conclusion: Future Direction

Omvedt G. 1995. *Dalit Visions: The Anti-caste Movement and the Construction of an India Identity*. New Delhi: Orient Longman.

Index

191